AF505934

POLITICAL RESPONSIBILITY AND THE EUROPEAN UNION

Manchester University Press

POLITICAL RESPONSIBILITY AND THE EUROPEAN UNION

Myrto Tsakatika

Manchester University Press
Manchester and New York
distributed in the United States exclusively by Palgrave Macmillan

Published by Manchester University Press
Oxford Road, Manchester M13 9NR, UK
and Room 400, 175 Fifth Avenue, New York, NY 10010, USA
www.manchesteruniversitypress.co.uk

Distributed in the United States exclusively by
Palgrave Macmillan, 175 Fifth Avenue, New York,
NY 10010, USA

Distributed exclusively in Canada by
UBC Press, University of British Columbia, 2029 West Mall,
Vancouver, BC, Canada V6T 1Z2

British Library Cataloguing-in-Publication Data
A catalogue record for this book is available from the British Library

Library of Congress Cataloging-in-Publication Data applied for

ISBN 978 0 7190 7515 5 *hardback*

First published 2008

17 16 15 14 13 12 11 10 09 08   10 9 8 7 6 5 4 3 2 1

Typeset by Special Edition Pre-press Services
www.special-edition.co.uk
Printed in Great Britain
by CPI Antony Rowe Ltd, Chippenham, Wiltshire

Contents

To Kaiti and Giorgos

Preface

This book goes to press at a time when the constitutional debate in the European Union (EU) seems to be coming to a close. What started in grand style with sombre speeches in the Constitutional Convention ends in fatigue and disenchantment after the rejection of the Constitutional Treaty in popular referenda and the compromise reached with the Lisbon Treaty. Nonetheless, a major puzzle is left unresolved: why are citizens sceptical towards the legitimacy of the exercise of authority in the EU and what would it take to address their concerns?

The main intuition that led to the idea of writing this book was that neither one-off attempts at institutional engineering nor centuries of cultural integration would provide answers. Recent developments seem to confirm this initial thought. We need to look at the diverse social and political practices that Europeans are being exposed to, are exchanging and are learning to share and the moral content of these practices. This is the stuff of which political community is gradually and concretely being built in Europe. And it is against the background of political community thus conceived that citizens' concerns can be addressed.

Acknowledgements are due to the Alexander Onasis Public Benefit Foundation for funding my postgraduate studies throughout the period 1998–2002 during which part of the research incorporated in this book was conducted. I am grateful to Albert Weale and Lynn Dobson who read and commented on previous drafts of chapters of this book. Exchanging thoughts and arguments with each of them has been intellectually stimulating and a great pleasure. Friends who patiently endured discussions on political responsibility and the EU over the years include Andrea Zhok, Havi Carel, Helena Rovner, Marcus Vossel and Vasso Karageorgiou. I would like to thank them for that patience.

Much of the book was written in a small fishing village on the Greek island of Samos overlooking the Turkish coast, during the summers of 2006 and 2007. Quite apart from the peace and beauty of the landscape which greatly contributed to my being able to see the project through, there is a lot to say for thinking about political community from the valuable perspective of a place that stands on the EU's external border. When the 'other' is only a swim's length away, one is not tempted to forget that the limits of community are always constructed, fluid and elusive.

Finally, my family – in particular my parents – have constantly and generously supported and encouraged me to complete this project throughout the past decade. This book is dedicated to them.

Myrto Tsakatika, Glasgow
January 2008

Abbreviations and acronyms

BENELUX	Belgium, Netherlands and Luxembourg
CFSP	Common Foreign and Security Policy
CoG	Chiefs of Government
CM	Community method
CONNECS	Consultation, the European Commission and Civil Society database
COREPER	Committee of Permanent Representatives
COSAC	Conference of Community and European Affairs Committees of Parliaments of the European Union
CSDP	Common Security and Defence Policy
DG	Directorate General
ECB	European Central Bank
ECHO	European Community Humanitarian Office
ECSC	European Coal and Steel Community
EMCO	Employment Committee
EMU	Economic and monetary union
EP	European Parliament
EPC	Economic Policy Committee
EPP	European Peoples' Party
ESDP	European Security and Defence Policy
EU	European Union
FM	Foreign Minister
GAC	General Affairs Council
GP	Green Paper
IGC	Inter-Governmental Conference
MEP	Member of the European Parliament
MP	Member of Parliament
NE	Nicomachean ethics

NGO	Non-governmental organisation
NP	National Parliament
OLAF	European Anti-Fraud Office
OMC	Open Method of Co-ordination
PES	Party of European Socialists
PM	Prime Minister
QMV	Qualified majority voting
RoP	Rules of Procedure
SPC	Social Protection Committee
ToA	Treaty of Amsterdam
TEU	Treaty on European Union
WG	Working Group

Introduction

The resignation of the Santer Commission

On 16 March 1999, for the first time in the history of the European project, the twenty-member College of Commissioners resigned before the end of its term. This took place under the presidency of the former Prime Minister of Luxembourg Jacques Santer, after the submission to the European Parliament (EP) of a Report by a Committee of Independent Experts, working under the auspices of the Parliament and the Commission, which substantiated allegations of fraud, mismanagement and nepotism. The Report came two months after a motion of censure tabled by the EP, which failed to come through, though not without showing that a large proportion of MEPs had lost confidence in the Commission. The shower of accusations was followed by a hostile press, which widely cited the following passage from the Report of the appointed independent experts:

> It is becoming difficult to find anyone who has the slightest sense of responsibility. However, that sense of responsibility is essential. It must be demonstrated, first and foremost, by the Commissioners individually and the Commission as a body. The temptation to deprive the concept of responsibility of all substance is a dangerous one. That concept is the ultimate manifestation of democracy. (First Report, 1999: 144)

The first signs of tension between the Commission and the EP were seen in the procedures that led to the appointment of the Commission President, Jacques Santer, in 1994: his leadership was not widely accepted, as became apparent in the narrow margin by which he won the vote that confirmed his investiture. With 262 votes in his favour, 244 against and 24 abstentions, he was the weakest president in the history of the institution (Hix and Lord 1996: 65). The Parliament thus expressed its discontent with the governments' choice of Santer over Dehaene, a deliberate choice of someone who would be less 'adventurous' and easier to deal with after the expansive leadership of Jacques Delors (Peterson 1999: 51).

At that stage, the criticisms mostly concerned policy orientation. However, as the term of the Commission progressed, the focus of criticism turned more towards issues of implementation and administration, since there were complaints and suspicions regarding the behaviour and performance of particular Commissioners, and stories were being circulated about particular instances of corruption in the Commission's administrative corps. There had also been alarming reports from the Court of Auditors, which alerted the Parliament's Budgetary Control Committee to a series of irregularities (Macmullen 1999: 703–4).

In 1998, tensions between Commission and Parliament were running high, leading to confrontations in the Parliament and culminating in the handing out of confidential information regarding fraud to the leader of the Greens by á Dutch Commission official, Paul van Buitenen, who was frustrated by the lack of progress that was being made against the Commission on these issues. By the end of the year, the Parliament voted against discharging the budget. Although the Treaties do not consider this an automatic show of no confidence, the Commission had made it clear that in a case where the budget was not discharged it would treat it as such and would demand that a motion of censure be tabled against it. In January 1999, the motion of censure was put to the vote and was lost, after hard national lobbying and among disagreement within European parliamentary groups. There were two failed attempts of censure: one against the two individual Commissioners who were the main target of discontent, Manuel Marin and Edith Cresson, and one against the College of Commissioners as a whole (Macmullen 1999: 706).

The motion of censure did not pass, but it became apparent that the Commission as a whole, its president and, especially, two of its members had been discredited, and allegations were looming without having been officially investigated. Huge questions were left unanswered, while the publicity that the issue received added to the importance attached to clarifying the matter. During the proceedings of the motion of censure, Santer promised internal reforms and agreed to assist the work of a Committee of Independent Experts that would investigate the charges and to accept its findings. All the Commissioners would assist the work of the independent experts, and access to all information and documentation would be granted.

The Committee was to be composed of senior officials familiar with auditing, law and European affairs and to report by March (which it did). Its task would be to:

> establish to what extent the Commission as a body, or Commissioners individually, bear specific responsibility for the recent examples of fraud, mismanagement or nepotism raised in parliamentary discussion. (First Report 1999: 9)

What were these areas of responsibility? The four categories of 'reprehensible conduct' that the Committee sought to investigate were: irregularities in the sense of actions or omissions that resulted in breaking established rules; fraudulent behaviour by way of intentional acts or omissions aimed at illegal benefit; 'ethically reprehensible behaviour', such as nepotism or favouritism, even if it did not involve fraud or irregularity; and 'serious and persistent infringements of the principles of sound administration'. The latter category referred to independence, level of public interest, account-ability and openness to the public (Macmullen 1999: 708).

What were the findings of the Committee of Independent Experts? In its investigation of the five files of policy implementation that it under-took – the Tourism Unit, the Med programme, the European Community Humanitarian Office (ECHO), the Leonardo programme and the Nuclear Safety programmes for Eastern Europe, it became apparent that fraud, irregularities and mismanagement had occurred, but that the Commission-ers in charge had no direct active involvement; they were, however, deemed guilty of omissions, since in claiming that they had not known what was going on in their departments, they admitted to serious failures. Once they had found out about the problems, they failed to act on time and to set up the appropriate control mechanisms. Moreover, they did not inform the other members of the Commission of problems that they eventually discovered and they were not frank about them in their dealings with the Parliament (Macmullen 1999: 712–13). On the case of the Security Office of the Commission, irregularities in the way the contract to run it had been assigned were discovered, and the president himself was criticised for failing to supervise his staff on the way they handled the matter. Finally, out of the seven accusations of favouritism that were investigated, three were seen to be acceptable (concerning the wives of Commissioners Liikanen, Marin and Pinheiro), one unsubstantiated (regarding business dealings of the Santer couple in Luxembourg), two bordering on irregularity (the appointments of personal friends and relatives of Commissioners Pinheiro and Wulf-Mathies) and, finally, one was seen to be a clear case of nepotism, regarding the appointment of Commissioner Cresson's personal friend, Mr Barthelot, as scientific adviser to the Commission when he was not qualified and had not produced any work for the Commission. It became clear that he was being paid with the Commission's money to do the personal political work of Ms Cresson in the town of Chatelleraut, where she had remained mayor until the end of 1997 (Macmullen 1999: 711).

The problem

To say that in the European Commission it was 'difficult to find anyone with the slightest sense of responsibility' is a serious accusation. What was expressed in the dramatic tones used in the Committee's report was the importance with which responsibility is endowed in the context of our politi-cal morality and the abhorrence felt in its complete absence. What is missing when political responsibility is missing? What is it that makes responsibility highly desirable in politics? To say that responsibility is 'the ultimate mani-festation of democracy' is not to say very much. Responsibility is valued not only in democracies but in non-democratic forms of governance as well. Responsibility is valued not only in the conduct of elected or appointed politicians but also in that of public officials, political groups and citizens. It is expected of not only public agents but also private firms, lobbies and non-governmental organisations. Finally, responsibility concerns not only the way in which political agents exercise their powers but also the way in which political institutions organise the exercise of these powers. Responsibility is a fundamental aspect of all political activity.

The accusation that all the members of one of the principal institutions of the European Union (EU) were lacking in political responsibility revealed a deficit quite distinct from the so-called 'democratic deficit'. It revealed the need for a discussion whose focus would not be democracy, justice or efficiency in the operation of the European Union; rather, the main concern of this discussion must be political responsibility itself and its actual and potential failure – or failures – in the EU. The responsibility deficit appears to be a significant aspect of the EU's lack of legitimacy. It must be seen whether the irresponsible behaviour of the Santer Commission was an exception, a bad episode in the history of the EU or, on the contrary, the first manifestation of crisis due to a more general phenomenon that concerns not just the Commission but the entire European system of governance; whether it reflects not only the failures of political agents at the European level to act responsibly but also the failures of responsibility that stem from the way in which institutions are set up in the EU.

Overview of the argument

If the EU fails in terms of responsibility to the extent implied by the Committee's report, it is necessary to understand why and how this came to be and why it is important that the problem should be dealt with. What exactly is political responsibility, why is it an important feature in any system of governance, and why should its absence trouble us? Finally, it is necessary to think about what can be done about it and what needs to change if the problem is to be addressed.

Chapter 1 will go back to the beginnings of the European project and try to trace the origins of the problem. From a historical–sociological institutionalist point of view, it will examine Jean Monnet's thought and strategy for European integration, whose influence, as it will be shown, was and continues to be dominant in the building of the Union. It will be argued that the problems of political responsibility that the Union faces today have their origins in the rationale behind the Monnet method of integration, which was grounded upon a technocratic conception of legitimate governance, normatively justifiable in terms of a particular notion of political responsibility: a set of qualities that ought to characterise those persons who comprise the technocratic elite that is meant to run a system of governance. It will further be argued that Monnet's conception of legitimate governance was problematic because the empirical and normative assumptions that informed it were unsustainable, as well as because the notion of political responsibility that was at its core was conceptually problematic: it was focused on the responsible qualities of leaders and blind to the institutional preconditions of responsibility.

Chapter 2 will show why it is important that the problems of political responsibility in the EU are addressed. This will be done by taking up the conceptual analysis of the notion of political responsibility and by discussing why political responsibility is desirable in governance, where governance is understood as a practice. In the context of a communitarian account of legitimate EU governance, which places responsibility in context alongside other aspects of legitimacy, it will be shown that political responsibility can only be achieved if both political agency and political institutions meet certain requirements in the practice of governance. On the agency side, the requirement concerns a set of political virtues: reliability, trustworthiness, consistency and prudence. On the institutional side, it refers to the ongoing and effective operation of accountability and the adequacy of identifiability and openness. Through the lens of an approach inspired by the work of Alasdair MacIntyre, it is argued that the desirability of the virtues of political responsibility lies equally in the exercise of those virtues as such, and in that such exercise in turn enables the achievement of predictability, order and stability, which are key goods 'internal' to (necessarily achieved through) governance seen as a practice.

The purpose of accountability is to encourage the development of the virtues of political responsibility, while identifiability and openness make accountability possible. This is not to say that they will be sufficient, but politically virtuous agency is much more likely to be encouraged and the legitimacy of EU governance therefore promoted if accountability and its preconditions are present than if they are not. Chapters 3, 4 and 5 will therefore examine accountability, identifiability and openness in the EU, focusing on the impact of key recent changes introduced in the institutions of the EU after the European Constitutional Convention, the Constitutional Treaty and the Lisbon Treaty. The emphasis will be on such developments as the new state of affairs in the executive involving the introduction of the office of a long-term Union President and High Representative, the new role for national parliaments as guardians of subsidiarity, new provisions for openness in the Council, the issue of simplification, and others.

The concluding chapter will summarise findings in Chapters 3, 4 and 5 and will attempt to provide answers to the following questions: to what extent are accountability, identifiability and transparency developed in the Union's institutional make-up – in short, to what extent is there a responsibility deficit in the EU? Can the Constitutional Treaty and the Lisbon Treaty be expected to improve or further worsen the responsibility deficit? Finally, if the Monnet conception of legitimate governance has indeed been at the root of the responsibility deficit all along, are there signs of its losing its prominence in the fifteen years that have followed the post-Maastricht legitimacy crisis?

Approach and methods

The last fifteen years have witnessed an unprecedented growth in the scope and range of the EU's decision-making. In some quarters, expansion has been coupled with the rise of popular scepticism and elite concern for the legitimacy of European governance. In the context of what has been termed the 'normative turn' in EU studies (Bellamy and Castiglione 2003), a lively academic debate over questions of democracy, diversity, citizenship, justice and rights in the emergent European political order is in full bloom (Weale and Lehning 1997; Beetham and Lord 1998; Føllesdal and Koslowski 1998; Lord, 1998; Weale and Nentwich 1998; Banchoff and Smith 1999; Eriksen and Fossum 2000; Hoskyns and Newman 2000; Bellamy and Warleigh 2001; Moravcsik 2002; Dobson and Føllesdal 2004; Lord and Magnette 2004; Weale 2005; Dobson 2006; Føllesdal 2006; Føllesdal and Hix 2006; Lord and Harris 2006; Smismans 2006; Attucci and Bellamy 2007; Ruzza and de la Sala 2007; Tsakatika 2007a). Normative political theorists have made valuable contributions, while EU scholars have become considerably more attentive to the problems raised. The aim of this book is to contribute to the contemporary normative debate on the legitimacy of EU governance by drawing attention to one of the more neglected issues pertaining to it, that of political responsibility.

The logic of normative argument is not about whether that or the other description of reality is true or false, or more or less accurate than another. Nor is it about how we can know whether one way of describing reality is more or less valid than another. Rather, normative arguments are arguments about why things ought to be one way rather than another; why one particular conception of things should be preferred over another. Their aim is, first, to demonstrate which normative assumptions, basic principles and theoretical traditions lie behind particular descriptions of reality and, second, to provide reasons why we should prefer one set of assumptions, principles or traditions over another when approaching that particular reality. This is what we attempt when we discuss political responsibility as an important component of 'good governance' in the EU.

Normative arguments are theoretical arguments, but theoretical arguments do not come from nowhere; we must assume empirical material when advancing them. In other words, we cannot construct theoretical arguments or proceed to conceptual analysis appropriately without making certain empirical assumptions. We could argue that a world run by red dragons would be better than a world run by humans, but we would probably have trouble finding any empirical evidence to support this argument. In this book the effort has been made to take empirical material into account and thus to make the conceptual and theoretical argument robust with respect to empirical assumptions. In particular, empirical studies about the EU as a system of governance, its history, institutions and policies have been widely consulted and taken into account throughout the course of the argument.

1

European Union in perspective: the legacy of Jean Monnet

Introduction

This chapter will attempt to provide an account of why the EU system of governance presents such serious shortcomings in terms of political responsibility. It will start by going through the principal theories of European integration, in an effort to see what kinds of explanation could be derived from them with regard to the EU's alleged failures of political responsibility. Neo-functionalist, liberal intergovernmentalist and new institutionalist approaches will be shown to yield different accounts.

By adopting a historical–sociological institutionalist framework, this chapter will go on to show, more specifically, why the problems of political responsibility in the EU emerged: it will look at the legacy of Jean Monnet, whose ideas and methods for European integration will be shown to have exerted a strong influence upon the building of Europe. The main question that will be addressed is whether there was something in Monnet's system of thought and action that could have caused problems for the development of political responsibility in the EU, insofar as the rationale behind his approach was influential in the building of the Union.

Firstly, it will be shown that Monnet's system of thought and action incorporated a *target* (the establishment of a novel system of governance), a *strategy* to arrive at this target (an incremental functionalist strategy) and a *conception of legitimate governance* ('responsible technocratic' governance). Secondly, the extent to which Monnet's system of thought and action have been influential in the development of the EU will be pointed out. Finally, it will be argued that Monnet's conception of legitimate governance was problematic and that the adoption of the rationale behind his plan is at the root of the failures of political responsibility that the Union faces at present. In particular, it will be argued that the problem with Monnet's conception of legitimate governance lies in the empirical and normative assumptions behind it, as well as in the notion of political responsibility that it employed. Insofar as Monnet's conception of legitimate governance was influential, its shortcomings can be shown to be reflected in the EU's shortcomings of political responsibility.

Neo-functionalist, liberal intergovernmentalist and neo-institutionalist readings of European integration

The neo-functionalist reading of European integration, as formulated by Ernst Haas in the 1950s, predicted a gradual, incremental process, characterised by 'spill over'. Incoherence and uneven development across the various sectors of interaction would only be temporary, as interdependence among sectors would lead to co-operation across the board with the purposeful interventions of key political and economic actors. Furthermore, the process was meant to be linear: no turning back could be envisaged once the multiplicity of national and supranational actors whose complex web of interaction was meant to give flesh and bones to the integration process had been mobilised and engaged in co-operation. Interdependence, the real driving force behind integration, would not be a reversible trend: it could best be described as a stream that grows inescapably into a massive river (Haas 1958; Lindberg 1963).

However, things did not turn out according to these early neo-functionalist predictions. The apparent lack of progress that characterised the process of European integration in the 1960s and 1970s seemed to discredit neo-functionalism and discourage neo-functionalists (Rosamond 2000: 85–8). Neo-functionalist work throughout this period was on the defensive, with many theorists modifying, correcting and refining their models of analysis, trying to explain why the initial predictions had not been met and moderating their claims to automatism (Schmitter 1996). More recent reformulations of neo-functionalism focused on developments in integration in the legal sphere (Burley and Mattli 1993), or on the changing economic structures that have enabled supranational actors to forge ahead with European integration in the 1980s (Sandholtz and Zysman 1989). Furthermore, some consider theories of 'multi-level governance' and policy networks analysis to be neo-functionalism's 'theoretical cousins' (Pollack 1996: 429). These approaches claim to discern the emergence of a European polity with strong supranational institutions, which interact with transnational networks of public- and private-sector groups within domestic political arenas and which are gradually overwhelming and disempowering national governments (Peterson 1995; Marks *et al.* 1996).

The 1990s saw the emergence of the 'liberal intergovernmentalist' approach to European integration, put forward by Andrew Moravcsik (1991, 1993, 1995, 1998). According to Moravcsik, there is nothing gradual or automatic about European integration: it is clear that decisions are made by Member State Chiefs of Government (CoG), whose preferences are articulated through struggles in their domestic political arenas and which bargain with each other over the terms of co-operation at the European level (Moravcsik 1993). The process of integration reflects the will of national leaders (Moravcsik 1998: 4). European supranational institutions such as the Commission, the European Parliament (EP) and the European Court of

Justice have only the power that has been delegated to them by the Member States (Moravcsik 1995) and are in any case kept 'on a short leash' (Pollack 1996: 429). Not only has there been no irrevocable sovereignty loss of the nation states to supranational European institutions, but co-operation at the European level has strengthened the nation states, or rather, it has strengthened nation state governments in their domestic politics *vis à vis* the societies over which they govern. Moravcsik has described European integration as a process of 'fits and stops', where the main events were 'grand bargains' between the nation states, followed by periods of 'consolidation', in the context of which national governments delegated the planning, organisation and realisation of what had been agreed to supranational actors, albeit keeping them under control (Moravcsik 1993: 473).

Naturally, the liberal intergovernmentalist story has not been without its critics. In a 1995 *Journal of Common Market Studies* article entitled 'Institutional Interaction and European Integration: Towards an Everyday Critique of Liberal Intergovernmentalism', Daniel Wincott argued that Moravcsik's analysis underplayed the autonomous power of the Union's supranational institutions. Grand bargains may well have been possible only because in the periods of 'consolidation' it was the supranational institutions that prepared the ground, devised policy innovations and informally channelled the agenda in certain directions (Wincott 1995: 602–6). In the same article, Wincott posed the institutionalist question: if institutions matter, why can national institutions have an impact on European policy outcomes while the institutions of the European Community cannot? (Wincott 1995: 602).

There is not one single institutionalist story to be told about the EU, but many. Rational choice institutionalist analyses of European integration emphasise the role of institutions as constraints to the strategic behaviour of rational actors, whose preferences are formed exogenously (that is, independently) of institutions. Their understanding of European integration is one in which not only states but also supranational actors interact strategically and where member states adopt (European) institutions which consequently constrain and direct their behaviour (Pollack 2001: 222). Rational-choice institutionalists have concentrated on analysing the influence of Europe's supranational actors with respect to the operation and outcomes of European institutional processes in order to see whether and to what extent they do indeed have autonomous influence, using formal models (Garrett 1992, 1995; Garrett *et al.* 1998; Tsebelis 1994; Pollack 1997; Tsebelis and Garrett 1997; Kreppel 1999; for a comprehensive review see Dowding 2000). They use principal-agent analysis in order to explain the autonomous power of supranational institutions, where the actors involved are understood to be exploiting the imperfect division of powers in the EU in order to increase their influence (Aspinwall and Schneider 2000: 13). Any set of institutional arrangements, including the present ones, can be conceptualised as a reflection of the relative influence of strategically oriented national and supranational European actors at a given moment in time. The preferences, loyalties, or identities of national or supranational actors continue to be formed *independently* of the institutional set-up of the EU.

On the other hand, sociological institutionalists ('reflectivists' or 'constructivists') understand EU institutional arrangements as the framework in the context of which preferences, behaviours and identities are shaped. The implication here is that preferences, behaviours and identities of both national and supranational actors have already been and could in the future be *transformed* as the process of institutional evolution continues its course (Sandholtz 1993; Wind 1997; Christiansen *et al.* 1999). We could envisage a European future in which national preferences converge, where new, common behavioural and social norms are constructed and where a European identity emerges. We could, however, just as well imagine a European future that is less 'European' – where national identities are reinforced, norms and behaviours diverge further, supranational institutions become empty shells and the term Europe signifies nothing more than the name of a continent.

Paul Pierson's historical institutionalist analysis is worth mentioning as an example of an institutionalist analysis of the EU which not only tries to take a middle ground among rational choice and sociological institutionalist approaches but also tries to provide a synthesis of neo-institutionalism with other theories of European integration. For historical institutionalists, institutional evolution cannot be placed under tight control as it is not an 'efficient historical process'. In other words, institutions do not turn out as intended by those who set them up but take on a life of their own. Thus, institutions are no longer subject to the control of those who set them up. On the contrary, those who did set them up find that their choices are constrained by these same institutions. 'History creates context, which shapes choice' (Aspinwall and Schneider 2000: 16). In the case of European integration, institutional and policy reforms that were indeed intended by national governments can be seen to end up transforming the preferences of the same, initially dominant, national actors in unintended, unanticipated, or even undesired ways, over time.

Pierson claimed that neo-functionalist explanations overstate the autonomous power of supranational actors; national governments, acting together in Council, remain the strongest actors in the European picture (Pierson 1996: 125–6). He conceded, in other words, that the liberal intergovernmentalist starting point is correct: states do indeed initially make agreements through bargaining, but after the initial bargain has been struck and after delegation of authority to supranational institutions has taken place, the autonomy of national governments to bargain will be more limited the next time around and will diminish each time a bargain is negotiated.

According to Pierson, significant gaps emerge between the institutional and policy preferences of national governments and the actual functioning of the institutions for a variety of reasons: because the supranational European institutions (European Commission, European Court of Justice and EP) are, at least partially, autonomous and try to enhance their autonomous power; because national decision-makers have short-term time horizons which are given by the next domestic general elections and may not pay much attention to long-term consequences of decisions concerning institutional and policy choices; because even if decision-makers do focus on long-term effects, there are likely to be unintended consequences in a complex system such as the EU, which are likely to take the forms of 'overload' or 'spill-over'; and finally, because the preferences of national governments as such change over time.

Once gaps emerge and national governments lose control, it is often not possible to reverse the process. The reasons mentioned by Pierson are: the resistance of supranational actors which may take advantage of gaps to strengthen their positions, institutional and legal barriers to reform, and sunk costs that make policy reversal unattractive. Governments get 'locked in' to policy options that they would not initiate if they were to start afresh (Pierson 1996: 131–48).

Pierson's analysis is not the only version of a historical institutionalist analysis of the EU to have been put forward: others have highlighted the role of culture and ideas within institutions such as the Commission (Armstrong and Bulmer 1997). Ideas can be said to be 'built into' institutional structures, which could favour certain policy choices and outcomes over others. By extension, the persistence of these ideas can systematically privilege some actors over others, thereby creating power asymmetries. An example cited by Armstrong and Bulmer was that, since European policy is market-oriented and since in the Commission there are separate consumer and producer Directorates-General (DGs) with shared competence over policy-making, the result may well be a persistent marginalisation of non-market interests (Armstrong and Bulmer 1997). Such versions of historical institutionalism can be said to be closer to sociological institutionalism, whereas Pierson's can be said to be closer to rational-choice institutionalism, given that his actors are, in the end, rational actors and not passive bearers of ideological or cultural biases (Aspinwall and Schneider 2000: 17).

The emerging historical institutionalist story of European integration is dominated by the 'stickiness' of institutions, which tend to persist in time and to increasingly circumscribe the choices that actors can make both in strategic and in substantial terms (Hall and Taylor 1996). This presumably counts for national governmental actors as much as it does for European supranational actors. To point out that, in this context, ideas and culture matter and can be seen to be built into 'sticky' institutions, could be argued to complete and enrich the kind of historical institutionalist analysis of the EU that Pierson undertakes. Taking into account the particular ideas, norms and cultures that are built into Europe's national and supranational institutions, there might be a better chance of identifying and explaining the strategic (or non-strategic) behaviour of the actors involved, in the context of specific episodes in the history of the EU, as well as the overall, long-term process of integration from a historical institutionalist perspective.

Despite the deep differences among the various institutionalist approaches to the EU, it can be argued that they all share some characteristics.

First, they all agree that institutions matter, and that, therefore, the study of the EU should focus on the study of the institutions involved in its governance (Checkel 1998).

Second, in principle, *all* institutions matter: institutionalist analyses claim not to be biased towards the supranational or the national institutions (as are, respectively, neo-functionalism and liberal intergovernmentalism) but to adopt an empirical approach in order to see which institutions do in fact matter and how (Wincott 1995: 602).

Third, institutionalist approaches are argued not to imply a *telos* for European integration, neither in the direction of supranational union nor in the direction of strengthened state dominance; rather, any prediction must be localised, contingent on the empirical study of institutions and always medium-term (Bulmer 1997: 6).

Fourth, where neo-functionalism and liberal intergovernmentalism have tended to see the relationship between domestic and supranational institutions in the EU in terms of a zero sum game, institutionalist analyses tend to examine the interplay and mutual influence between levels in the EU context (Jupile and Caporaso 1999).

Fifth, institutionalism has been argued to signal a turning away from 'grand theory' towards the study of the day-to-day politics of the European Union (Bulmer 1997:16).

Theories of European integration and political responsibility in the EU

From the traditional neo-functionalist perspective, the EU could not be said to present any serious problems of political responsibility. Political responsibility, along with most other political questions, would be postponed to a distant future in which Europe would have evolved into a polity and where political decisions of a constitutive nature would have to be made. It would be pointless, in other words, to ask European politicians to behave responsibly and be aware of their obligation to assume responsibility or to demand fully operational practices of accountability in an emerging entity that was to be in a process of constant piecemeal evolution and whose agents would be members of various national and transnational elites, the role of which could not be characterised as strictly 'political'.

More recent neo-functionalists would argue that the EU is a *sui generis* polity, that we cannot view it in the same light as a state or an inter-governmental organisation and that we need to judge it as it is, looking at its novelty and unique advantages as well as what we understand to be its disadvantages. Such judgements may result in our thinking that we need to reconsider the way in which we conceptualize political responsibility or accountability in the EU context in a way that is different from the state-centric view we normally adopt when we think about such matters (Banchoff and Smith 1999: 7). In short, for neo-functionalists, old and new, the EU is not up against any problems related to political responsibility because political responsibility as we know it is not a principle that, at least for the time being, or in more general terms, is or should be applied to it.

A liberal intergovernmentalist would identify concrete problems of political responsibility in the EU. They would accept that while political responsibility for decisions taken at the European level lies at the national level in full, national governments can often escape parliamentary accountability and scrutiny, given that domestic oppositions are disadvantaged in terms of the information they can obtain about what their respective governments do in 'Brussels' and given that these governments are able to blame 'Brussels' for their own decisions. It would seem that the EU's responsibility deficit, as identified from a liberal intergovernmentalist point of view, appears as a national problem which can only find national solutions. The shortcomings of political responsibility in Europe are a problem for national publics and national groups, which see their control over their respective governments concerning European issues (and also by extension national issues) as continuously diminishing. Political responsibility could be strengthened at the national level: more openness, more political debate and more accountability for national governments with regard to European issues could improve the situation in terms of political responsibility in the EU as a whole.

However, this is not a line of argument that can be taken very far. European-level co-operation has meant a strengthening of CoG positions in two ways: a better environment for bargaining with one another and an improved position in the context of their domestic social and political arenas. Among the reasons that national governments have for agreeing to co-operate with one another, a significant one is that their position of power is improved *vis à vis* their citizens; thus their hand is freer at decision-making, both domestically and at the European level, since they can escape from having to account for their actions. If this is an integral part of why national governments agree to co-operate at the European level, increased accountability at home would mean less or no integration for Europe. It seems, therefore, that liberal intergovernmentalism entails a trade-off between political responsibility and European integration: we can either have responsible national governments or irresponsible European governance.

Rational-choice institutionalist accounts would lead us to a similar picture with regard to political responsibility in the EU. For liberal intergovernmentalists, where responsibility lies and the lines of accountability in the EU are clear: all responsibility lies with national governments; the problem is that national governments can escape national scrutiny because their domestic publics do not have access to information about EU decision-making. This capacity to disown responsibility is an important motive for national governments to co-operate at EU level. Rational-choice institutionalists not only acknowledge that the locus of political responsibility and the lines of accountability in the EU are blurred but also show that, in many cases, supranational actors are irresponsible *vis à vis* their (presumably irresponsible in their turn) national principals.

According, then, to the liberal-intergovernmentalist and rational-choice institutionalist accounts, the EU does present shortcomings in terms of political responsibility, which are mainly to do with the difficulty national principals have of keeping their supranational agents under control. While this perspective can help to trace the origins of the problem of political responsibility, it is not sufficient as it addresses only one part of the problem, which has to do with certain aspects of accountability.

A historical–sociological institutionalist approach can provide a more comprehensive explanation of the Union's responsibility deficit. The ideas, norms and aspirations that were built into the original institutional structure of the EU can be shown to have had a decisive influence upon it throughout its evolution. All actors on the European stage cannot help being constrained in their choices, both substantively and strategically, by the inheritance, inertia, or 'path dependence' of European institutions and the ideas, norms and aspirations that are built into them, however much the latter have, in their turn, evolved over time.

Adopting the historical–sociological institutionalist perspective, in the greater part of the rest of this chapter it will be argued that the ideas of Jean Monnet, who is (not by chance) called the father of European integration, have been decisive for the development of what have been identified as the characteristics of the EU system of government, as well as its problems in terms of political responsibility. Monnet's intellectual and practical–political formation took place in a specific historical and institutional context. He had clear ideas about what he wanted the European project to become, was active in strategically pursuing his ideas and succeeded in exerting consider-able ideational influence in the setting up of the original European institu-tional structure and upon the way in which this structure has evolved.

Institutions are 'sticky': they tend to persist. So it has been that the origi-nal European institutions have evolved with considerable continuity. The High Authority of the European Coal and Steel Community (ECSC), Jean Monnet's brainchild, was none other than the ancestor of today's European Commission. The Commission's role in the European institutional structure has been a key role with a significant impact upon the development of the entire European project (Tsakatika 2005). Finally, institutional evolution is not an efficient historical process. Indeed, not all of what Jean Monnet intended the European project to become is, after all, what it actually has (so far) turned out to be.

The aim of Jean Monnet: an experiment in governance

In the aftermath of the Second World War, the European continent was devastated by the loss of millions of human lives and by the extent of destruc-tion in economic activity and infrastructure. The Cold War, the result of division among the major nations of the winning alliance, cast a menacing shadow over future prospects. In the early 1950s, key actors in Western Europe decided that the path to unity would be the best way of securing the terms of reconstruction, maintaining peace and delivering prosperity to the peoples of this part of the continent. It was these aims that informed the vision of Jean Monnet, well-known to be the founding father of European integration.

Jean Monnet was not a professional politician, an academic or a war hero; he was a Frenchman from the Charente region, who, starting from doing his part in the family business by selling brandy abroad, became involved in international trade and finance, worked for the League of Nations, devised the French post-war reconstruction plan and finally went on to become the founder of the European Communities.

The challenge was how to pursue the aims of maintaining peace and creating prosperity in Europe. Monnet had understood – long before the war, as it emerges from his *Memoirs* – that the achievement of one aim would not be possible without the achievement of the other. From the point of view of the international economic system, European nation states were too small to survive and compete. With France in mind, Monnet wrote:

> The countries of Europe are too small to give their peoples the prosperity that is now attainable and therefore necessary. They need wider markets … To enjoy the prosperity and social progress that are essential, the States of Europe must form a federation or a 'European entity', which will make them a single economic unit. The British, the Americans and the Russians have worlds of their own into which they can temporarily withdraw. France is bound up with Europe. She cannot escape. (Monnet 1978: 222)

A great deal has changed since then, but the point remains unmistakably relevant. In order to secure prosperity, a unitary European economic system would have to be created. Nation states that had fought each other not only during the (then) recent Second World War but many times before in the past would have to join hands and gradually merge their economies. This would mean that fundamental aspects of the sovereign state as we knew it would need to be abandoned. It was not only that the fragmentation of economic activity in nation-state units in Europe was not profitable; it was also dangerous. There were strong reasons to believe that it was the attachments to nation states that had brought about two destructive world wars to the continent in no more than half a century. By uniting economically, European countries would take the direction of prosperity, and at the same time, this union would strike a decisive blow to the very concept of the sovereign nation state. The objective was, in other words, not only economic but also political in a revolutionary sense (Kohnstamm 1990: 8).

Monnet's target was the creation of a system of European governance; a system that would provide the economic space for the European countries to recover and prosper, secured under a regime of peace. This kind of governance had never been tried before; it was an experiment. This is because both the goals it set out to achieve and the way in which it proposed to achieve them were unprecedented. And the experiment began successfully in the early 1950s, when the governments of the first six European Community countries – Belgium, the Netherlands and Luxembourg (Benelux), together with France, West Germany and Italy – under the personal influence of Jean Monnet, decided to pool their resources of coal and steel, thus promoting structural changes in the economic map of the area. The ECSC was established in 1952, and its High Authority was meant to be:

> a strong executive authority, whose primary function would be developmental and which would act by enforcing a code of industrial good conduct. While seeking the advice of unions and other 'constructive' elements, the new directorate was to regulate business through competition, pricing and investment policy, and conduct joint buying and selling; as such it was intended to operate in a manner opposite to that of cartels. Where they existed to protect profits the new High Authority … would encourage productivity; where private producer arrangements operated secretly, it would use open covenants; and where they were run by private managers in the service of private interests, it would be an agent of the public weal. (Gillingham 1991: 139–40)

The High Authority would not be run by politicians of the European nation states; it was designed to be a body of experts and administrators, who would come from the nation states but act independently of them and be loyal to the European idea. They would initiate proposals and have the authority to issue regulations binding on the Member States within the High Authority's field of competence. Monnet would be its first president. An Assembly of national parliamentarians and a Court of Justice on the one hand and a Council of Ministers on the other would act, respectively, as democratic and judicial safeguards and representatives of the Member States at the European level, but the High Authority would have the central role. Although the ECSC was not a flamboyant success if it is assessed against the specific targets it set out to achieve, it did indeed initiate the process of European integration (Gillingham 1991: 152–8). It did, in other words, initiate the novel system of governance that Monnet had in mind.

To summarise: Monnet's target was the establishment of an innovative system of governance, meant to secure lasting prosperity for Europeans by creating a viable economic unit to replace a multitude of unviably small economic units and a lasting peace amongst them by the overcoming of national rivalry through the building of supranational co-operation. The ECSC was to be the first step towards the establishment of this system of governance, and its High Authority, made up of high-ranking, independent, European-minded administrators and experts, was to be the central agent of this development.

Monnet's strategy: step by step

There has never been a declared consensus on one single predetermined plan for Europe, with a beginning, a middle and an end, although a multitude of such plans has been proposed (Marks 1997: 25–7). The steps towards unity have depended greatly – in both substance and detail – on the balance of power and national interest among the member states, on the degree to which their leadership has been favourable and on international context, as well as on the ideas and timely interventions of single or small groups of European-minded individuals. However, what is clear is that the way in which European integration has proceeded has consistently been characterised by a particular pace: it has proceeded and continues to proceed in a fashion that is not linear, consistent or all-embracing; rather, it has been forged in a trial-and-error, piecemeal and unpredictable fashion.

It is not by accident that European integration has proceeded thus. Looking back to its early stages, it is not difficult to distinguish the blueprint, or rather the 'method', that was envisaged to carry it through. This method, novel in its conception and implementation, has proved itself to be durable enough to persist for fifty odd years. This is none other than the Monnet method of integration. Europe, he writes in his *Memoirs*,

> 'will not be built all at once, or as a single whole: it will be built by concrete achievements which first create *de facto* solidarity'. (Monnet 1978: 300)

What was meant by 'concrete achievements'? Monnet was convinced that once people and, by analogy, the European States through their representatives are shown their common interests – that is, from the point of view of a third disinterested party, their 'objective' common interests – they will come to see the light and will agree to co-operate on the basis of exactly what is profitable and fair for all of them.

> Without a doubt, the selfishness of men and of nations is most often caused by inadequate understanding of the problem in hand, each tending to see only that aspect of it which affects his immediate interests. But if each interested party in those circumstances, instead of facing another party with opposing interests, is presented with the problem as a whole, there can be no doubt that all parties' points of view will be modified. Together, they will reach a solution that is fair. (Monnet 1978: 83)

The way to unite Europe, in other words, would be to show the states their common interests and convince them to act on these interests, pursuing them on a permanent basis. Concerted action was to be a 'concrete achievement' insofar as there was continuity and institutionalisation of the common projects that would result from it.

Integration would be a long process, and states, as well as people, would have to get accustomed to it gradually. How was this to be achieved? Monnet was a functionalist: he considered economic, not explicitly political, co-operation to be fundamental in binding the states and the citizens in Europe together. For this reason, 'concrete achievements' would need to be economic ones first, although not only economic, in the long term. This approach ruled out the strategy of giving priority to political grand designs of a constitutional nature at this early stage of integration:

> [H]owever urgent political union may be, and however great the progress already made, it does not seem possible to by-pass the requisite stages. The political union of tomorrow will depend on making the economic union effective in the everyday activities of industry, agriculture and government. (Monnet 1978: 431)

Monnet had faith in the automatism of 'spill-over': the functionalist idea that once co-operation starts in one field of socio-economic activity, it will become necessary in other, neighbouring fields as well. A holistic approach would therefore be out of the question, at least for some time. His strategy was incrementalist: For example, it would not be on 'economic policy' (generally speaking) that states would begin to co-operate but on specific economic sectors, as happened with coal and steel first, atomic energy a few years later, agriculture even later, and so on; and this on the basis of specific common projects. States, citizens, associations of industry, agriculture and organised labour would have to be shown the concrete advantages of co-operation, through specific projects involving specific sectors. Thus, *de facto* solidarity among elites and citizens would result.

How would the continuity of these projects be guaranteed until the time was right to take further steps towards integration? Monnet, in his *Memoirs*, could not have stressed more strongly the importance of setting up common, supranational institutions that would organise, oversee and co-ordinate the common projects and that would set them to work and see them through. He believed deeply in the necessity of establishing institutions at the European level because through them individuals and groups would be gradually habituated into new, European routines.

Monnet thought that individual action and institutions were inexorably linked: 'Nothing is possible without men: nothing is lasting without institutions' (Monnet 1978: 304). Institutions are beneficial for humans because 'human nature is weak and unpredictable without rules and institutions' (Monnet 1978: 37). Humans – as a species – have a short memory; their experience is necessarily shorter than that of institutions: 'recurrent situations make it necessary to recall the same common sense rules that men continually forget. Hence, incidentally, the need for institutions to establish the framework of rules for action, and substitute an enduring collective memory for fleeting and fragmented individual experience' (Monnet 1978: 457). Institutions embody collective memory:

> The union of Europe cannot be based on goodwill alone. Rules are needed. The tragic events that we have lived through and are still witnessing may have made us wiser. But men pass away; others will take our place. We

cannot bequeath them our personal experience. That will die with us. But we can leave them institutions. The life of institutions is longer than that of men: if they are well built, they can accumulate and hand on the wisdom of succeeding generations. (Monnet 1978: 384)

In that sense, institutions allow us not to make the same mistakes. They also provide the ground for us to make the best of our abilities: The new European institutions would be 'the only vehicle through which Europeans could once more deploy the exceptional qualities they had displayed in times past' (Monnet 1978: 392–3). Institutions exert their influence upon men and women by moulding their common habits and ways of working. They make change a smooth process by gradually changing these habits when this becomes necessary.

Institutions, provided that they have been well built, accumulate and pass on the wisdom of succeeding generations (Monnet 1978: 384). Once established, institutions become stronger than people: they 'have their own strength, which is greater than the will of men' (Monnet 1978: 469). These institutions would become the centres of European activity, and vague 'amounts' of sovereignty would gradually be delegated to them by the national centres.

Monnet's 'method' or strategy for arriving at European integration was characterised by incrementalism; his faith was placed in the functionalist notion of 'spill over'. He believed that the taking of small concrete steps in the form of common projects backed up by common institutions would result in the building of the system of governance he had in mind and would create *de facto* solidarity among European peoples.

The normative underpinnings of Monnet's plan

In the building of a European system of governance, Monnet did not just have a precise goal and strategy in mind; he was also convinced that this system of governance would be better, and therefore more acceptable in normative terms, than other alternatives that were, if not available, at least imaginable at the time. In other words, he entertained a notion of *legitimate* governance. This section will seek to discover which conception of good governance lay behind Monnet's plan and will attempt to reconstruct his conception of legitimate governance, which can be argued to be justifiable on the grounds of a specific notion of political responsibility.

As mentioned earlier, the impetus for European governance would be given by a European technocracy. The High Authority of the ECSC was to be its institutional embodiment. An Assembly and a Court, as well as an intergovernmental body comprised of national governmental agents, would certainly complete the institutional picture, but the High Authority would have the central role. The group of experts appointed from the Member States that would compose it (in dialogue with interest groups and other non-governmental actors) would provide the advice upon which governments and men of politics would act (Featherstone 1994: 154). Expertise would be politically neutral since it would have to take the objective view. 'Politics' is meant here as partisanship, party politics, confrontational politics or ideological politics. Good governance in those terms was understood to be technocratic, neutral or politics-free governance (Tsakatika 2005).

Furthermore, legitimate governance would be governance by an elite of ability and would therefore be exclusive and meritocratic. Monnet insisted on hand-picking his associates for the High Authority, selected on the basis of merit, because the body of guardians had to be composed of the very best. The main interaction of his technocratic elite would be with other elites – national, subnational and 'European' – which would have to be convinced and to stand behind the same European cause that motivated the technocratic elite. Clearly, in contradistinction to the early years, European Commissioners have increasingly been persons who, in addition to their ability, have political backgrounds, either national or European (or both), to draw from (MacMullen 2000: 49); they are not technocrats in a strict sense. This does not change the fact that they continue to be chosen principally for their ability to handle portfolios and they are obliged to take an oath of independence *vis à vis* member state governments (Nugent 2001: 21–2).

Given that the process of integration would be a business of elites, it would not involve citizens directly. Priority would not be given to openness, disseminating information and explaining and debating European issues with, or in the presence of, citizens. Rather, the aim was to convince and involve other elites. There would be no seeking to convince citizens through open debate before asking them to agree or consent to the European project; instead they would be 'tricked' into new habits and projects through living the benefits of concrete achievements. In other words, legitimate governance did not mean giving priority to the creation of a European public sphere (Habermas 2001).

Closely related is Monnet's idea of weakening national sovereignty without directly confronting it. It would be through a multitude of different projects that vague amounts of sovereignty would pass on to a European centre. No one would ever really know just how much sovereignty was being transferred from the nation state level to the European level. Furthermore, it was not very clear what this European centre would look like. Despite the fact that Monnet placed great emphasis upon the role of European institutions, which would be the centres of European governance, he did not consider that these institutions would be unalterable or stable in principle:

> Gradually, other tasks and other people would become subject to the same common rules and institutions - or perhaps to new institutions: it was too early to say. (Monnet 1978: 393)

In other words, legitimate governance did not necessarily include a clear and stable centre of power and, consequently, it did not require clear accounts of who did what and when – that is, a clear allocation of tasks.

The European technocracy would be 'independent' from the Member States in the sense that it would not be influenced by them in its operation (for instance when they applied pressure to satisfy their particularistic interests), either as individuals or as a group, and would not be accountable to them in a political sense. Independence would imply a transfer of loyalty from the national to the European level. This transfer of loyalty would, in effect, be guaranteed by the superior intelligence of the technocratic elite: they would be able to *see* the common interest and this would win them over and induce them to work for its enforcement. (This common interest, however, would not be articulated in terms of a common morality, values or identity; it would be the common gain resulting from the more efficient handling of common affairs achieved by taking an overall view). Being convinced of a greater efficiency would be the primary motivation, and this would come before any other motivation – for example loyalty to one's country or to a political ideal, or even loyalty to a European idea that went beyond Europe as a more profitable level at which to handle common affairs. As for accountability, the High Authority would surely not be able to do miracles without the agreement of the nation state governments, but it would set the agenda and take the initiatives. The technocrats of the High Authority would not be accountable for what they put on the agenda and they would not be accountable politically, since their proposals would be made in the name of greater efficiency and not from a political partisan point of view. Legitimate governance, then, for Monnet, was independent (from nation state influence) and politically unaccountable (to national governments and citizens) governance that would appeal to citizens because it would be efficient.

In summary, Monnet's conception of legitimate governance was technocratic, elitist and unaccountable. At the same time, it gave no space to the creation of a public sphere and it did not provide for a clear allocation of political tasks at the European level. What made Monnet think that this kind of governance would be legitimate? It is obvious that he placed a lot of faith upon the members of the technocratic elite that would initiate, sustain and develop the project he had in mind. He thought of them as the guardians of the European project. He insisted (as has been mentioned) on hand-picking his associates for their exceptional qualities and their commitment to the European project. It can reasonably be argued that the exceptional qualities demonstrated by the members of his technocratic elite would provide the justification, if any could be provided, for his conception of legitimate governance. In other words, it was those qualities at the centre of his conception of legitimate governance that would justify its superiority.

Which qualities did Monnet require of his associates? The High Authority, later the European Commission, would initiate policy and be the 'motor of integration'. Its members would have to be relied upon to keep going even when the momentum for integration on the part of the member states was slow or non-existent. Reliability, then, was a necessary quality. The other task of the guardians would be to build trust, where there was mistrust, from a position that presupposed that the guardian body itself was to be trusted on grounds of the merit of its European-mindedness. Trustworthiness was therefore a required quality. Furthermore, Monnet's maxim was: 'look at the problem as a whole and in the light of the general interest' (Monnet 1978: 83). The guardians would need to be able to take the overall view; to distinguish the overall as opposed to the partial and the long-term as opposed to the short-term interest (Duggett 2000: 80–1) and to act upon it. In other words, the guardians would have to exercise their power with coherence and prudence. The body of guardians would be small in order to be flexible. Monnet wanted to keep it small, because he did not want it to turn into a 'bureaucracy', meaning that he wanted a body that was flexible enough to act efficiently as one body and be well equipped to design policy and make decisions, not a vast duplication of national administrations (Monnet 1978: 373). Above all, then, the guardians would have to be efficient.

The picture that emerges from the qualities that Monnet expected of his associates is one of responsibility; the guardians would be 'responsible' and this would be justification enough for the form of governance that he advocated. They would be able to govern better than politicians, because politicians looked after the partial view, that of their nation states. Politicians were subject to re-election and therefore to short-term interests; they could not be relied upon to carry out the project at all and they would not do it efficiently because they would be too busy bargaining and clashing over national interests (Beetham and Lord 1998: 16–17). The best alternative was clear for Monnet: it can be summarised as responsible, technocratic governance.

The influence of Monnet's ideas upon the development of the EU

There are few cases where one person's ideas can clearly be said to have exerted a strong influence upon key political outcomes. Founders of political regimes and constitution-makers can be considered as such. Here, we might add the inventors and practitioners of political methods, like Jean Monnet. Did Monnet's thought really have such a great influence upon the development of the EU?

European governance is multi-level on a permanent basis: although struggle has featured (and continues to do so) in the relationships among the different levels, the balance between them has the nature of a constant dialogue, which is conducted on the basis of co-existence, mutual compromise and intradependence. It has not been the case so far that one level has signalled the end of the other, or that it seems likely to do so in the foreseeable future. Important decisions are taken at all levels and one cannot have the full picture of what is happening at one level without seeing what happens in the others (Weale, 2000a: 12–13).

Federations as well as confederations are by definition multi-level systems of governance. However, at a certain point, the balance of power among the different levels of governance becomes agreed upon and settled one way or another. This does not mean that changes are not made, or that the covenants that regulate the balance of power are – or should be – treated as sacred texts; rather, when there are changes to be made, this is done by public agreement in the form of constitutional reform or by the signing of another treaty. This is not the case in the EU. The balance of power between the different levels of government is constantly under negotiation in a way that most of the citizens involved do not keep track of. We know that the European system of governance is multi-level, and we know that there is a certain balance of power between the different levels, but we do not know exactly what this balance is at any given moment.

The unstable relationships between the different levels of governance, as well as between the actors that operate at the same level within the system, give rise to an issue that is fundamental for any system of governance: they raise doubts about the balance of power and authority, the allocation of tasks and the limits of jurisdiction among the main actors of the system. Furthermore, they raise doubts about the distribution and the delineation of responsibility within the system: it is not always clear who is supposed to do what and when.

If European governance is in this state of affairs today, it is not by chance. Monnet's functionalism can be shown to have played a significant role. Monnet was opposed to firm political statements that would crystallise and stabilise the system. He did not want a constitution to be drawn up, at least, not before the process of 'spill over' had progressed significantly. On the one hand this was a strategic move, which was intended not to provoke opposition from national forces that would feel threatened. On the other hand, there was a theoretical bias behind this position. The functionalist idea that social and economic activity can and should come before politics ('concrete achievements' first, politics later, in the EU case) was certainly a determinant.

Had someone told Monnet that the result would be a weakness in the allocation of power and responsibility, he would have answered that the 'spill over' process would have automatically provided socio-economic integration in the long term and that formal political concerns were not to be discussed until that process had gone far enough. This being the case, the balance of power was left to oscillate between a federal and a confederal type, in the hope that at a certain point necessity would automatically make it tend towards the European level.

Furthermore, governance in the EU is horizontally complex: at each level of governance there is a variety of actors that have a say in the policy-making and decision-making processes. In other words, to speak only of the European level, it is not only the main institutions (the Commission, the Council and the EP) that play a part in the process of governance; it is also a series of mixed committees, NGOs, agencies, media, experts and interest groups that take part in the same process (Weale 2000a: 12–13). As the European edifice has grown in complexity, the networks of policy and decision-making have grown with it. Complexity has grown not only vertically, because the balance of power among levels of governance is unstable, but also horizontally, because the balance of power among the institutions at the EU level is unstable. The powers of the EP, for example, have continued to grow, particularly since its first direct election in the late 1970s, and this has continued to overturn the balance of power. It is said that the flux at the level of institutions encourages the development of networks (Peterson 1995: 82, 86–7). Network development, in other words, is a response to the complexity of the system, to which the networks in turn add. This, indeed, seems to be a permanent feature of the system of European governance.

Horizontal complexity gives rise to another problematic aspect of EU governance from the point of view of responsibility: it is often impossible to understand who is to blame when something goes wrong, and therefore, it is virtually impossible to attribute responsibility (Kohler-Koch and Rittberger 2006: 41). Networks of governance may be useful and desirable for other reasons – for example, for their ability to generate legitimacy and consent of leading elites and groups of experts through mutual consultation, or for their ability to disseminate information. Nevertheless, for political purposes of attributing and apportioning blame, this system can prove detrimental to the point of doing away with public trust and confidence. It therefore becomes difficult to develop effective practices of accountability (Eising and Kohler-Koch 1999).

Openness and transparency are also made difficult. Networking involves a constant dialogue between small and/or large groups. Even in the best of cases, where all information that is circulated in networks can be made freely and publicly available in sufficiently simplified form, it is not an easy task to process and understand it. The obvious result of these problems of horizontal complexity is the mystical nuance that the utterance of 'Brussels' has acquired and the vague suspicion of conspiracy that accompanies it.

Monnet's intellectual and personal influence is here crucial. From the beginning, Monnet's corporatist–elitist project sought to involve a multiplicity of actors in networks that would support European policies and projects. In functionalist terms, these actors were to be the glue that would consolidate European governance. This was how he operated while he was the president of the High Authority of the ECSC, and this is also how he continued to operate as head of the Action Committee for the United States of Europe, between 1955 and 1975. It was at the core of his understanding of social action that a multiplicity of actors and elites would spin the web of governance.

Finally, governance in the EU tends to be characterised more by a bargaining than a problem-solving style of decision-making. In the problem-solving style, what is important in achieving effective agreement among different parties is appealing to a set of common values, whereas in a bargaining style the appeal is made to the individual self-interests of all the participants. In the case of the former, the ultimate sanction is exclusion; in the case of the latter, sanction is organised in terms of individual incentives (Scharpf 1988: 258–9). Where bargaining prevails, it is assumed that the parties involved will pursue their self-interest, while agreement will take place only if the benefits it is expected to deliver are at least as high as those to be expected from not participating. Where problem-solving prevails, a view to the common interest is already established, forming the ground of co-operation. Self-interest on behalf of the parties to the agreement is not an issue, 'either because individual interests are submerged in the common interest, or because they are effectively neutralised through institutional arrangements separating the pursuit of common goals from the distribution of costs and benefits' (Scharpf 1988: 260). Whereas in bargaining, non-agreement is perfectly acceptable in terms of the surrounding norms, in problem-solving, to be seen unwilling to co-operate in order to reach agreement would involve disapproval and disloyalty before the joint undertaking (Scharpf 1988: 260).

In the EU, what is lacking is the view of the common good, or the perception of a common identity, which would support appeal to common values and allow for short-term sacrifices from particular members in situations where this is necessary for long-term common benefits to result. This becomes obvious when one considers the extensive and elaborate bargaining over funds and policies that takes place whenever national ministers and prime ministers meet in Council or European Council formation. Is bargaining, however, a permanent decision style for European governance? According to Scharpf, it is not impossible for the norms associated with bargaining to evolve into 'communal' norms, and this would stand more chance of happening if economic conditions were steadily favourable. In that case:

> the common enterprise is clearly a positive-sum game from which all are profiting. And if it is possible to establish agreement on common criteria for the distribution of benefits and contributions under these benign circumstances, there is at least a chance that the agreement might hold even when the nature of the game changes to zero-sum or negative-sum. (Scharpf 1988: 262)

The prevalence of the bargaining – as opposed to the problem-solving – style of decision-making haunting the Union most certainly does not encourage the development of a European political debate, which would be necessary for the attribution of political responsibility at the European level. The politics of bargaining are politics of secrecy: the bargaining parties have every interest in concealing, or in not revealing, what they have given up in order to get something else that is higher in their priorities of self-interest. What does the common interest consist of? That is a question that in internal member state politics is supposed to be decided through public contestation or through public agreement; at the European level it becomes an issue for the executives to decide on their own. The setting of priorities does not become subject to public debate. Moreover, the fact that appeal is made to self-interests, rather than to common values or common interests, goes against what the encouragement of an open European public debate would require. In order to discuss our common problems and set our common priorities, we must have reason to believe that problems and priorities are common. Europe is still in that sense pretty much a Europe of national executives which 'bargain out' agreements on partial policies away from the European public eye.

Monnet sought to create trust among the national elites that he worked with because he realised that this would be the only way in which they would understand and agree to pursue their common interests yet also make unilateral 'sacrifices' when these were necessary in order for long-term common interests to be achieved. He thought he could do this just by bringing them together and persuading them to see these common interests. However, he did not appeal to a common 'identity' or to a common set of values but showed them that it would be more beneficial to co-operate than not to co-operate; on the other hand, his appeal was directed only at elites, not citizens, for whom trust-building assumed a secondary importance to be achieved in the distant future through seeing in everyday life – again – that being in Europe was better than being outside of it. The process of integration was not meant to involve citizens directly through open public debate and democratic choice.

It has been argued that Monnet's ideas and strategy had an important influence upon the formation of the core characteristics of European governance and, therefore, upon the problems of political responsibility that these characteristics create. This is not to say that we can attribute everything that the EU was, is or will be to Monnet's ideas; it is only to say that his ideas played a significant part in the formation of certain characteristics of the European experiment in governance and in generating the problems of political responsibility to which these characteristics have given rise.

In the next section, an attempt will be made to answer the question that naturally arises at this point. Monnet's thought and strategy were influential in the development of the EU and its problems of political responsibility, while his conception of legitimate governance was indeed justified in the very terms of the qualities of political responsibility. Was there something wrong either with Monnet's notion of responsibility or with his conception of legitimate governance?

The problem with the normative foundations of the Monnet plan

Altiero Spinelli, a prominent figure among Europe's committed federalists, was quoted as saying that 'Monnet has the great merit of having built Europe and the great responsibility to have built it badly' (Burgess 1991: 55–6).

Monnet's plan, which incorporated a target, a strategy and a conception of legitimate governance, seems comprehensive and coherent. He wanted the establishment of a novel system of European governance designed to deal with the problems of maintaining peace and creating prosperity in the long term for the peoples of the continent. He had a functionalist–incrementalist strategy in order to achieve it. Finally, he had a conception of legitimate governance and a normative argument based on political responsibility to back it up. How is it then possible that, after half a century, the European Commission, the direct descendant of his High Authority, came crashing down after being discredited on counts of – of all things – lack of responsibility? It will be argued here that the problem lies with Monnet's conception of legitimate governance: firstly, the normative argument and the empirical assumptions that lay behind it were unsustainable, and secondly, the notion of political responsibility at the core of it was conceptually inadequate.

To begin with the first problem, the Monnet normative argument in favour of 'responsible technocratic' governance can be reconstructed as follows: technocrats are more responsible than political agents, therefore, technocrats should govern. The first step of the argument (that technocrats are more responsible than political agents) can be understood in the sense that technocrats are best positioned to be responsible; they are more able to take the overall view and can be more counted on to pursue it than political agents, who are by definition partial – to a party political ideal or to the national ideal – because they articulate, represent and advocate a partial point of view. The second step of the argument (that technocrats should govern, or that legitimate governance is technocratic governance) depends on the sustainability of the first step. If the first step of the argument is unsustainable, or if it is shown that there are serious doubts about its sustainability, then the entire argument becomes unsustainable. In what follows, it is argued that indeed the first step of the argument cannot be sustained.

Is it the case that technocrats are generally more able to take the impartial and overall view than political agents? With respect to impartiality, we cannot argue against the view that we attribute to Monnet, that political agents are generally partial; it is indeed the case that they represent political parties, advocate political ideals and articulate political views and interests, despite the fact that occasionally politicians have been able to rise above partiality and express themselves on behalf of the 'nation', the 'common good', or the 'general will', when the circumstances have required it. However, it can be argued that technocrats are not necessarily impartial. Technocratic governance may well lead to capture by particular interests, or, technocratic elites may have their own (partial) interests to pursue. Furthermore, the pursuit of efficiency in governance may be advocated as an impartial ideal, but this impartiality may be questioned when one asks to whose benefit, or in the pursuit of which goal we are to consider governance efficient. With respect to taking the overall view, the case is much stronger against Monnet's view:

technocrats are experts, so they are meant to be specialists, not generalists of governance. Political agents on the other hand are more likely to have some sense of overall problems or interests, even if they will advocate their own partial account of the overall problem and its overall solution.

The argument that technocrats are more responsible than political agents, then, cannot stand. But why did Monnet trust technocrats more than politicians? How did he come to adopt the empirical assumption that technocrats are generally more likely to demonstrate the qualities of responsibility than political agents? Jack Hayward claimed that Monnet was

> 'accustomed to the manipulation of politicians whose expectancy of high office in any government was likely to be short-lived and of bureaucrats more inclined to inertia than innovation'. (Hayward 1996: 252)

Monnet's general preference for governance by a technocratic elite, in other words, stemmed from his experience of the Fourth French Republic and the operation of the French Planning Commission, which he headed after the war (Page 1997: 5). Monnet experienced the instability and inefficiency of the governance of France due to the radical and conflict-ridden parliamentary politics of the time, and he sought not to inflict the new European project with those shortcomings. Instead, he favoured governance by a small group of experts, because technocratic governance had been, in his view, the central stable, long-sighted and 'responsible' element throughout the Fourth French Republic (Duchêne 1996: 51–3). It is possible that his experience of the Fourth Republic led him to assume that selected technocrats were more likely to be responsible than political agents.

To experience a situation where instability and inefficiency reign because political circumstances are exceptional and political life is turbulent, and where the qualities of responsibility are called for in order for governance to be effective and stable, is not to experience something unique. By contrast, to experience (or to believe to have experienced) a situation where the qualities of responsibility are the exclusive preserve of technocrats is rare and does not allow for easy generalisation.

It is not difficult to find examples of other, non-political agents and groups that have in the past exhibited the qualities of responsibility, or have claimed to have exhibited them, when all around them was in chaos: leaders of military *coups d'état* who seized power to prevent civil war or to provide stability; dissidents and intellectuals in East European countries who provided guidance to millions of people during the transition from the communist era; Italian magistrates who uncovered the extent to which the political class of the first Italian Republic was corrupt and did not hesitate to proceed to '*Mani pulite*'; and journalists who dared to uncover what political agents wanted to conceal. Technocrats are only one group among many that have, historically, shown themselves to be responsible where politicians have not.

What might be said is that all these instances, including the Fourth French Republic, where non-political agents have specifically demonstrated the qualities of responsibility were short lived and exceptional. And it might also be said that the rest of the time, it is from political agents that the qualities of responsibility are expected. It is not possible, in any case, to assert that technocrats have at all times and under all circumstances been more likely than political agents to demonstrate the qualities of responsibility or to expect that they will in the future.

It becomes clear at this point that Monnet's normative assumption that technocrats are more responsible than political agents is unsustainable both in normative terms and in terms of the empirical assumptions that inform it. Therefore, his argument that legitimate governance is 'responsible technocratic' governance is unsustainable as a whole.

There is a second major problem with Monnet's conception of legitimate governance, which is conceptual–theoretical and lies with his notion of political responsibility. Responsibility, in Monnet's scheme, is the substance of what renders governance legitimate; it is indeed legitimate governance itself. If the notion of responsibility that was derived from Monnet's scheme presents conceptual problems, then this will constitute a serious shortcoming of the conception of legitimate governance as a whole. Two problems with Monnet's notion of political responsibility will be pointed out: it is conceptually weak and it does not convince us of its value or desirability.

Problems such as the unclear allocation of tasks among the levels of governance of the Union, the difficulty in apportioning political blame, difficulties with the development of effective mechanisms of accountability, and the lack of openness and public debate are problems of political responsibility that are due to institutional design. In Monnet's notion of responsibility it would seem that such problems are not considered; responsibility is a property not of institutional structures but of agents, and it refers to certain qualities that characterise the individuals who compose the ruling elite and not to institutional features or organising principles of political systems. Furthermore, it would seem that Monnet's conception of legitimate governance fails to take into account – and goes against the development of – these institutional features or principles of political responsibility that are meant to organise a system of governance. It would seem, in other words, that Monnet's conception of legitimate governance, on the one hand, strongly requires the qualities of political responsibility but, on the other hand, is incompatible with what are generally understood to be the institutional features of responsibility.

It might be argued that these are simply two different notions of political responsibility. The literature points in this direction, without exception: we cannot talk about a single unified and distinctive notion of political responsibility; the latter can be described as a set of loosely related meanings that bear 'family resemblances' and that 'cannot be reduced to one essential meaning' (Bovens 1998: 24). But is it true that these two meanings of political responsibility are mutually exclusive? For Birch, this is not the case: there is no necessary conceptual tension between 'prudence' and 'consistency' in political action and accountability (Birch 1964: 17–22). Similarly for Pennock; what he calls 'an attitude characterised by rationality and morality' need not be in conflict with accountability and identifiability (Pennock 1979: 266–8). It will be argued that not only is there no tension between responsibility as qualities of agents and responsibility as organising principles of institutions but the qualities depend on the institutional features for their reproduction and maintenance; therefore, the two different meanings of political responsibility can be shown to be conceptually and practically interrelated.

When legitimate governance is rendered dependent upon the qualities of a small (or, for that matter, large) number of individuals, there must be a strong conviction that such individuals can be found and that, once found, they are willing to play this role. Moreover, such individuals will have to continue to be found and be willing to play the role in the future. What would happen when Monnet was no longer there to pick his 'responsible' associates? Who would pick them? Would there always be others like them around to take their place? Would they always be willing to play the role? It becomes obvious that, in the absence of appropriate mechanisms of selection (that is, in the absence of institutions that outlive the persons that are meant to operate within them), this would be highly unlikely.

At this point it can be argued that the High Authority was meant to be an organisation that would develop a culture of its own and its own institutional mechanisms of selection. Monnet was well aware of the role of institutions as mechanisms that habituate people into routines by generating rules of 'appropriateness' (March and Olsen 1984) and that continue to impose requirements upon people in accordance with those rules. However, between attributing the highest value to the qualities of responsibility in order to justify a conception of governance and claiming that institutions can in general be self-perpetuating in terms of the qualities they select, there is an intermediate consideration: the question of which would be the *particular* institutional mechanisms that the High Authority would have to develop in order to select in perpetuity those individuals endowed with the *particular* qualities of responsibility. Nowhere in Monnet's writing can an answer to this question be found. We take this to constitute a serious inadequacy not only in Monnet's notion of political responsibility but also in the discussion of the notion of political responsibility as a whole. Nowhere in the literature do we find an account of the notion of political responsibility that incorporates a clear analysis of both the substantive understanding of the qualities of political responsibility and the institutional mechanisms meant to reproduce them in an ongoing system of governance.

As will be argued extensively in the next chapter, it is not by chance that we consider accountability, the presence of a clear and stable allocation of tasks, and certain requirements of openness in governance to be elements or prerequisites of 'responsible' governance. And it is not a linguistic coincidence that we give the same name to a set of qualities on the one hand

and a set of institutional characteristics on the other hand. It will be argued that these institutional characteristics are necessary in order for the qualities of responsibility to be re-selected. Political responsibility will emerge as a requirement placed upon both agents and institutions.

It was not just that Monnet's conception of legitimate governance did not consider the institutions of responsibility to be necessary: his conception along with his strategy, insofar as they were influential, worked towards hindering their development. It was clearly shown that his conception of legitimate governance not only viewed the institutional mechanisms of accountability, identifiability and openness as unnecessary requirements but was hostile towards their operation. It becomes understandable that if political responsibility requires not only a set of qualities but also a set of institutional mechanisms to ensure the reproduction of these qualities, and if Monnet's conception of legitimate governance highlighted the qualities but was hostile to their sustaining institutions, then Monnet's notion of political responsibility has serious shortcomings. Furthermore, the desirability of the qualities of responsibility is not clear in Monnet's scheme. Why are those qualities valuable in the context of governance? We can only guess that the reason for Monnet's attribution of value to these qualities was related to his preference for stable and efficient governance. In such a reading, these qualities might not be good in themselves but would be good instrumentally for governance. However, this is not clear from Monnet's writings.

Conclusion

In this chapter, it has been argued that the rationale behind the plan of Jean Monnet, which had a strong influence on the building of the Union as it is today, can be seen to be at the root of the problems of political responsibility that the EU presents. Monnet's goal of creating a European system of governance, his incremental functionalist strategy and his conception of legitimate governance as 'responsible' technocratic governance have been examined. Monnet's intellectual influence upon the development of the Union and its consequences in terms of the problems of political responsibility that the Union faces have been shown.

Monnet's conception of legitimate governance was technocratic, elitist, politically unaccountable and hostile to openness and the creation of a public sphere. Nevertheless, it was justifiable in terms of the qualities of responsibility that the technocratic elite in charge of the system would be required to have. It has been argued that Monnet's conception of legitimate governance failed on three counts.

Firstly, the normative argument that sustained it – that is, the idea that technocrats are more responsible than political agents – does not stand up to scrutiny; the assertion that technocrats are more responsible than political agents is grounded on insecure normative foundations and false empirical assumptions.

Secondly, Monnet does not provide an account of why the qualities of responsibility are desirable in terms of legitimate governance. We can only guess that the reason for Monnet's attribution of value to these particular qualities was related to his preference for efficient governance. In such a reading, these qualities might not be good in themselves but would be instrumentally good for governance. However, this is not clear from Monnet's writings.

Finally, the notion of political responsibility that is at the core of Monnet's conception of legitimate governance is conceptually problematic. It fails to account for the reproduction of the council of responsible guardians or to see that it is through accountability, identifiability and openness that this reproduction can take place. To those aspects of responsibility, Monnet's conception of legitimate governance remains blind. Monnet's understanding of political responsibility, limited to a set of qualities possessed by a chosen few, appears inadequate in conceptual terms. But the general discussion on political responsibility also appears to be inadequate since it fails to account for the relationship between the two sides of responsibility.

The paradox of the Union having been built under the influence of a conception of legitimate governance that places the emphasis on responsibility and the extent of the problems of political responsibility that the Union is confronted with today is explained by the fact that Monnet's conception of legitimate governance was problematic in the first place and set the EU on a course that led it to accumulate a deficit of political responsibility.

We need not, however, conclude that political responsibililty is irrelevant to legitimate governance in the EU, that it is generally undesirable in governance or that it is in itself a problematic concept. Quite the contrary. As illustrated in the introductory chapter, the 1999 crisis, which did much to plunge the EU deeper into its crisis of legitimacy, was very much about the lack of political responsibility. The relationship between legitimate governance and political responsibility will thus be fully explored. The uproar caused by the Santer Commission's resignation was in fact about our valuing political responsibility in governance and thinking it desirable. There is all the more reason to attempt an in-depth analysis of the neglected concept of political responsibility and to examine why it should be desirable in governance. These tasks will be undertaken in the next chapter.

2

Political responsibility and legitimate governance

Introduction

The aim of this chapter will be to show what political responsibility refers to and why political responsibility is desirable in all systems of governance, including the EU. The two main ways in which political responsibility is understood – that is, as a set of qualities (or virtues) and as a feature or an organising principle of a system of governance will be examined and the relationship that binds them will be explored. It will be demonstrated that these are only two different aspects of the same phenomenon: political responsibility is a principle that calls for certain requirements to be met in an ongoing practice of governance and these requirements are placed upon both political agents and political institutions. To put this in other words, political responsibility is a principle of legitimate governance that refers both to how political agents should act and to how political institutions should be set up. It will be argued that political responsibility is a desirable feature for every practice of governance because it enables the achievement of predictability, order and stability. But before discussing political responsibility as a requirement upon agency as well as upon institutions of governance, it is first necessary to provide an account of the relationship between institutions and agency.

Institutions and agency

How are agency and institutions to be understood and how are they related? A concept that is often employed by the historical institutionalist school in order to characterise the relationship between agents and institutions is the notion of 'role', borrowed from sociology. Roles can be thought of as *animations* of social positions related to institutions and performed by their incumbents. The social positions to which roles correspond are linked internally by way of the purposes that institutions must serve and the modalities that are established to serve these purposes. The demands of a role 'consist of normative expectations, a set of quasi-moral duties to perform, entitlements to their performance and rights to criticise, complain and seek redress in case of failings' (Hollis 1994: 165–7). An agent then is seen as an incumbent of one or more roles, whose requirements may or may not always be compatible; each agent must employ practical reasoning in order to respond to the requirements placed upon them by their various roles to the best of their ability.

By exercising practical reasoning, agents can influence, but generally not completely rewrite, the role or roles that they occupy. The extent to which this can take place will depend on the extent to which their roles are flexible, or 'institutionalised' (Scharpf 1997: 62). Searing distinguishes between 'position' roles and 'preference' roles; the first are linked to positions that require the fulfilment of a specific number of specific duties, while the second are linked to positions that require fewer fixed duties and are therefore, as a whole, more flexible and more open to change. He cites as examples of each case a minister and a backbencher in the House of Commons, respectively (Searing 1991: 1249).

The less a role is institutionalised, the greater the extent to which that agency can alter the shape of the role. To take an EU example, Monnet's High Authority in the 1950s was a far more malleable institution than Barroso's European Commission of the beginning of the twenty-first century. However, if political agency has great room for manoeuvre, the damages (or benefits) that it can bring about to the performance of a system of governance may be significant. To take more EU examples, Charles de Gaulle's insistence in maintaining the national veto for important national matters in the 1960s damaged the functioning of the European Community by condemning it to decision-making impotence for two decades. Jacques Delors' dynamic Commission presidency was crucial to the completion of the single market and paved the way for economic and monetary union (EMU).

Virtues and practices

To the extent that agency can influence the workings and the make-up of institutions, it becomes apparent that if one is interested in the good operation of institutions, the performance of agency is important. Role incumbents differ as to the valuable qualities they can employ in the performance of their roles. These qualities may differ in degree, in kind or in both. For example, one role incumbent may be more reliable than another (difference in degree), or two role incumbents may be equally efficient, one through decisiveness and the other because of a conciliatory disposition (difference in kind). These qualities can be termed virtues, and if we care about the good make-up and operation of political institutions we will consider political virtues to be a desirable feature of political agency. The full spectrum of the valuable qualities, or set of virtues, that incumbents can demonstrate and employ in the performance of their roles can be described as their 'character'. A character is formed over time, it evolves around certain more or less stable and recognisable features and it generates certain expectations from those that see and deal with the role incumbent from the outside.

Virtues are not the sole preserve of individual agents; they can also be discerned in the action of collective bodies. It is not only individual incumbents of political roles, such as kings (in monarchies), religious leaders (in theocracies), or presidents, politicians, ministers, political leaders and citizens (in democracies) that demonstrate political virtues; it is also collective incumbents, such as the king's advisers, military and religious councils, government cabinets, political parties, parliaments, committees and groups. At this point an analogy can be drawn by treating collective incumbents like individual incumbents and by attributing to them political virtues, roles and role-related obligations.

Collective political bodies conduct their business with a certain internal division of labour. This division can be fairly complicated, but it does not have to be so; in fact, it can even be absolutely horizontal – a simple string of identical and interchangeable roles. This division of labour, shaped through time but progressively growing to a state of relative stability, generates working methods and routines and creates certain expectations for those who look to the collective political body from the outside. The collective incumbent's political virtues are discernible through the specific pattern of valuable qualities that emerges systematically from its internal workings. To take an example, a government can be characterised in various ways. First, it can be characterised by the way it reaches decisions: it can work as a group, with a prime minister (PM) who is *primus inter pares*, or in a more centralised way, with decisions depending more on the PM and his or her advisers. Second, it can be characterised by the timing of its interventions: it can wait to do all the good and pleasant things until just before election time or it can work a steady but firm schedule that will hopefully pay off at the end. Third, it can be characterised by the degree of its coherence before the public or by its decisiveness before considerable obstacles, and so on.

It is worth examining which qualities are virtues and why they are valuable as qualities. The content of what is considered a virtue is historically specific (Adkins 1960; MacIntyre 1981; Smiley 1992; Bovens 1998). Courage, for example, referred to bravery in war during Homeric times; nowadays, it may refer to changing one's well established but not fulfilling career at the age of fifty. What is considered a virtue now may not have been considered a virtue in the past, and vice versa. For instance, chastity may have been considered a virtue in medieval European Christianity, but this is no longer the case in many Western contexts. Furthermore, a quality that is considered a crucial virtue in one context may not be considered as crucial in a different context. Impartiality, for example, may be regarded as crucial for a judge when administering justice but not when the judge is at home helping children out with homework.

The virtues, then, are not universal qualities of character that are always to be considered as such, irrespective of the particular context within which the virtuous agent must act. More precisely, it is only from within a particular context that we can fully understand, appreciate and practise the virtues. We may know, for example, that to honour one's parents is considered a virtue in many cultures, but it is only from within each particular culture that we can fully understand what that entails in particular (Blum 1996: 233). The context in which the virtues can be approximated is what Alasdair MacIntyre has termed 'practices', which he defines as

> any coherent and complex form of socially established co-operative human activity through which goods internal to that form of activity are realised in the course of trying to achieve those standards of excellence which are appropriate to, and partially definitive of, that form of activity, with the result that human powers to achieve excellence, and human conceptions of the ends and goods involved, are systematically extended. (MacIntyre 1981: 187)

In the context of practices, there develop – among participants – particular relations, the nature of which is linked to the nature of the practice in question. The virtues, according to MacIntyre, reflect those valuable ways according to which we consider that these relations ought to be conducted.

MacIntyre defines what makes virtues valuable in the following terms:

> A virtue is an acquired human quality, the possession and exercise of which tends to enable us to achieve those goods which are internal to practices and the lack of which effectively prohibits us from achieving any such goods. (MacIntyre 1981: 178)

If the virtues enable the achievement of goods internal to (that is, necessarily achieved in the context of) practices, does that mean that they are merely instrumental to the achievement of these goods, and is their value exhausted in their being means to an end? For Aristotle, the possession and exercise of the virtues were (and were considered to be) valuable in themselves because what was good for man – the *telos* of man's life – was to live a virtuous life (Aristotle *NE*: 1097b22–98a27). Virtue, in other words, was a constitutive part of what was good, and this is what made it valuable in itself. Furthermore, apart from being good in themselves, virtues were *also* good because they were instrumental to the achievement of the good life (*NE*: 1100a34–b26). It was through practising the virtues that one achieved a good life. Virtue then was valuable both as a means and as an end; it was an ongoing human state that was part of, and at the same time led to, the good life. What is inescapable here is the Aristotelian commitment to the idea that man has a *telos*, that there is an essence of man that finds its expression and excellence in the virtuous life.

MacIntyre follows Aristotle in his understanding of virtues as, at one and the same time, means *and* ends (Mulhall and Swift 1992: 81). In terms of means, MacIntyre suggests that the virtues enable us to achieve goods internal to practices. In terms of ends, he follows Aristotle in considering them valuable in themselves as part of the good life, part of man's *telos*. However, MacIntyre's understanding of that *telos* differs from the Aristotelian understanding. MacIntyre acknowledges that in our time the idea of a *telos* for man would be unacceptable in biological terms and debatable in philosophical and historical terms. Even if we agreed that such a *telos* existed in historical terms, we would have a hard time agreeing on its exact nature. MacIntyre's claim is that although we cannot argue in favour of a *telos* for man in Aristotelian terms, we can argue in favour of a *telos* for man seen as the subject of history and practices. The good for man is the search for the good for man, MacIntyre says; and this means that what is good for man will be particular to specific types of man or woman acting in similar contexts (of historical period, society or practice) (MacIntyre 1981).

Goods internal to practices

Governance can be understood as a 'practice' in the sense that MacIntyre uses the term. It is complex, coherent, socially established and co-operative; and it is only in the context of governance that certain goods can be understood and achieved. And it could be argued that governance practices advance their own standards of excellence. In the light of MacIntyre's analysis of the relationship between virtues and practices, we might see that there are certain virtues that enable us to achieve certain goods 'internal' to (the practice of) governance. In this section it will be argued that key goods 'internal' to governance are predictability, order and stability.

Governance provides for predictability by organising expectations; it creates order through the establishment of coherent rules and the development of mechanisms for the enforcement of these rules, thus enabling co-operation and co-ordination; and it guarantees the stability needed for the pursuit of individual and collective projects.

Fame, money, or even power can be achieved outside of governance; such goods would clearly be what MacIntyre calls goods 'external' to the practice. Of the goods that can be said to be 'internal' to the practice of governance, common deliberation, participation, civic friendship, and the formation of a political culture might be said to fall into this category. But there are certain other goods that we can consider to be more fundamental, in view of the fact that if they are not achieved, governance could be thought to fail at a much more basic level than would be the case if the less fundamental goods were not achieved. It might even be said that in the absence of those more fundamental goods, the less fundamental ones would not be achievable at all in the context of the practice of governance. One set of goods 'internal' to governance that are of such key importance can be shown to be predictability, order and stability.

People need some measure of certainty in order to construct plans and carry out projects into the future: there would be less incentive to plough a field if there was a risk that a government official might later come to take away the crop for no publicly justifiable reason. Bearing children would be a painful enterprise if anyone were able to come and kill them on the following day. One might hesitate to acquire skills if one knew that one's services might not be required next week. Being able to count on nothing – or, in other words, radical uncertainty – is the enemy of worthwhile projects. A certain degree of predictability is necessary if any plans are to be made (Kay 1998: 22–3). Furthermore, people's projects, more often than not, depend upon co-operation with others, or at least co-ordination with others. In all kinds of spheres, from draining a swamp to common security and defence, as well as in health and education, or the building of major public works, co-operation is required. In order for such activity to be possible, rules and norms that enable co-operation or ensure co-ordination need to be developed, as do mechanisms to enforce them. There needs to be an assurance that, for the most part, others will do their share and will not impede others from doing theirs. Finally, common rules which provide the grounds upon which communication can take place must emerge, with common symbols, words and understandings that people can use to create new meanings and new projects. In short, order is needed if co-ordination and co-operation are to be made possible. Finally, for individual and collective projects to be possible, it is necessary to have the guarantee of a certain level of continuity, with the assurance that any changes in the established order will take place at a rate that people can keep pace with, that the rules will not change from one day to the next and that, when the rules do change, there will be adequate notice and a reasonable time to adjust. What is needed, in other words, is a degree of stability in order. Making projects – individual and collective – is the only way people have of extending their capabilities and their understanding of goods and ends, whether it is self-interest that motivates them or the desire to contribute to global justice. And in order to make projects people need the goods of predictability, order and stability.

It might be asked what is meant by 'people', or in other words, for *whose benefit* are the goods internal to governance. It is not difficult to say that – in the very basic sense that this was set out above – the subject needs predictability, order and stability just as much as the democratic citizen does. The same holds for those who exercise political authority: officials, ministers, non-governmental actors, private actors, democratic and non-democratic governments alike do nothing *but* make projects. To govern oneself is to make projects; to govern is to make projects *par excellence*. These projects, being of grand scale, need even more precision in their planning and in calculating their consequences; therefore, they need to count on the existence of predictability, order and stability to an even greater degree. It is, in other words, for all those who participate in the practice of governance that the goods of governance are goods.

The legitimacy of practices

The MacIntyrean approach employed here generates a distinctive understanding of the legitimacy of practices in general and of the practice of governance in particular, one that will be dubbed the communitarian account of legitimacy. What is meant by legitimacy of a practice here is its normative justifiability and consequent reasoned acceptability (Beetham and Lord 1998). The communitarian account of legitimacy is made clear once it is contrasted with liberal egalitarian and neo-republican accounts.

Liberal egalitarian accounts are more often than not deontological: they treat the legitimacy of governance as conditional on whether a set of institutional arrangements of governance conform to universal principles that would be agreed upon by free and equal moral agents acting under appropriate choice conditions (Rawls 1993; Habermas 1996). The presence of cultural, moral or other 'deep' community ties is not a precondition for there to be legitimacy of governance practices according to most liberal egalitarians, nor is a strong sense of political community; rather, it is universal rights and general rules ensuring rights that matter (Habermas 1995).

Liberal egalitarian approaches posit that the EU would achieve legitimate governance if it could be shown to be a just order; some of these approaches employ the social contract device (Lehning 1997; Attucci and Bellamy 2007). Liberal egalitarian accounts of the legitimacy of EU governance will often appeal to post-national rights of citizenship (arguing that there would be universal agreement among equals upon the desirability of such rights) and render legitimacy conditional upon the extent to which they are ensured procedurally or substantively by appropriate governance arrangements (Lehning 1997; Føllesdal 1998; Weale 2005; Dobson 2006).

Neo-republican accounts are often consequentialist insofar as they assess both the legitimacy of institutional or constitutional arrangements and the value of civic virtue according to their effectiveness in safeguarding the ultimate good for individuals: that of non-domination (Pettit 1997). As with liberal egalitarian accounts, republican accounts will not normally require the presence of deep communal ties – cultural, ethnic and linguistic – as background to legitimate governance. Rather, they will seek to accommodate the multiplicity and overlapping membership of diverse communities bound together by a strong civic bond that is formed through the active participation of citizens within the political realm, where rights are defined. The notion of community required for legitimacy here is political community.

Neo-republican accounts of legitimate EU governance emphasise polycentricity, plural and multi-level representation, extensive checks and balances, constitutional flexibility and federal arrangements in order to ensure that no individual or minority is dominated by others. Legitimacy will depend on the rule of law, appropriate constitutional arrangements and the development of civic attachments that, in turn, will be formed insofar as citizens feel that decisions and discussion about rights are made by them at the level most relevant to them – rather than being imposed upon them – while at the same time transnational attachments are encouraged (MacCormick 1997; Bellamy and Castiglione 1997, 2000; Chryssochoou 2002; Tully 2007).

In the communitarian account of legitimacy, a practice's legitimacy depends by and large on how well the practice works on its own terms – that is to say, on the extent to which the particular virtues flourish, the relevant internal goods are achieved and the related human ends and conceptions of those ends are extended in the course of striving for excellence. Insofar as practices are the sources of the standards of excellence they are the bearers of moral standards (Lutz 2004: 40–2) and therefore they include the canons of legitimacy of the practice. In other words, the criteria for evaluating the legitimacy of a practice are drawn from within the practice.

When it comes to the legitimacy of the practice of governance, the communitarian account requires that certain virtues, such as may be thought to comprise – in Western liberal democratic contexts – the virtues of responsibility, fairness, self-rule and solidarity, flourish within the practice. It also requires that the virtues in their turn enable the achievement of goods internal to the practice of governance, such as order, justice, democracy and equality. It follows that the virtues of responsibility and the internal goods (such as order, stability and predictability) whose achievement they enable are only one key set of virtues and goods internal to the practice of governance.

Both liberal egalitarian and neo-republican accounts appeal to external canons – either universal principles or desirable consequences – to assess the legitimacy of a practice. In the communitarian account by contrast, legitimacy is evaluated according to criteria internal to the practice. Furthermore, liberal egalitarian accounts do not render the possibility of legitimate governance conditional upon the presence of cultural or political community ties, whereas the neo-republican accounts require a strong sense of political community. In the communitarian account, legitimacy is embedded in particular communities, partially constituted by practices within which virtues flourish. These communities are moral communities, where one conception of the good is to some extent shared and exemplified by the virtues.

Two objections can be raised at this point against the communitarian account of legitimacy. At first blush it seems totally inappropriate to ground the legitimacy of EU governance upon community, whatever type of community that may be. Europeans do not share a common political or cultural identity (Smith 1992), nor do they share a feeling of common belonging that need not rely on ethnicity but must be strong enough to sustain majority rule and support practices of solidarity (Grimm 1995). Moreover, the EU cannot in any self-evident way be described as a moral community; on the contrary, it is extremely plural and diverse as to the conceptions of the good and the related virtues practised by its citizens. Therefore it is the wrong context to which to apply the communitarian account.

Secondly, even if the communitarian account could be shown to apply to the EU, it is problematic in itself, owing to the fact that the criteria for legitimacy it posits are internal to practices and therefore not amenable to independent scrutiny. In other words, the account comes up against the problem of 'evil practices'. These objections will be dealt with in the following two sections.

Community and the virtues

MacIntyre claims that the virtues can only flourish in small-scale, local communities (MacIntyre 1981, 1989, 1994, 1998). Yet he denies that there is anything special about local communities. What matters in his view is that, as in the Aristotelian *polis*, virtues can only flourish where citizens share a common understanding about the good of their community and strive to achieve it to the utmost degree (MacIntyre 1994). Two conditions make this possible. One is sociological: morality is exemplified through common activities and the good has a concrete practical content that all have unmediated access to. In contrast to larger communities, such as national or even supranational communities, the local community is bound together by face-to-face relationships, ties built through direct co-operation and personal commitments. It is thus the social unit that allows for the virtues to flourish *par excellence* because it incorporates the practical conditions for exemplifying and thus arriving at the common good (Blum 1996: 231–5).

The second condition is cognitive. People must be in a position to share perceptions of what is good, because they share common ways of speaking and understanding. This, MacIntyre argues, is easier to achieve when there is some degree of cultural affinity, although he makes it clear that he is not speaking of a Volk (MacIntyre 1998). Andrew Mason argues that MacIntyre's position can be interpreted to mean that virtues cannot flourish unless they are widely accepted as being such: if they are not, the context of practices within which virtues can be exercised disappears (Mason 1996: 196). Yet from MacIntyre's point of view, linguistic or cultural affinity alone will not suffice unless it is combined with the sociological condition. In his Lindsay Lecture on patriotism, MacIntyre argues that patriotism taken to mean attachment and loyalty to one's community may be a virtue, provided that the nation is understood to be striving for a higher ideal. However, without the sociological conditions, which are likely to be absent in nation states, this will only be empty of substance and potentially dangerous (MacIntyre 1984).

We can take MacIntyre's argument to be that face-to-face social relationships and ties of co-operation plus a degree of shared understanding are more likely to be found in small-scale, local communities. Therefore, virtues and practices are more likely to grow in such contexts. However, his evaluation of the possibilities for virtues and practices to actually flourish in even small communities is notoriously negative. It is MacIntyre's conviction that virtues are species about to become extinct because modernity has created unfriendly conditions for their survival. Liberal individualism has corrupted social ties and therefore the relations that are at the core of practices; the modern state has marginalised small-scale communities where the virtues can flourish and has condemned them to impotence; most importantly, a single overarching conception of the good is unavailable: conflicts about values, goods and ends are such and so many that they have become impossible to handle, thus irreparably fragmenting the moral unity of human lives (MacIntyre 1981).

If it is true that virtues are most likely to flourish in small local communities, national states would, as MacIntyre claims, be unfit to foster the virtues in general and those of political responsibility in particular; equally or even more so the EU. For in national communities the cognitive condition may be present, but the sociological condition is not, while in the post-national EU context neither condition holds. Above all, market values, weak social ties and a multi-plurality of conceptions of the good and the virtues deeply characterise the EU. If the virtues of responsibility are desirable in EU governance – in themselves and because they enable the achievement of order, stability and predictability and constitute (one set of important) canons for its legitimacy – then we are up against a serious problem: the EU does not seem to be a context in which the virtues of political responsibility can flourish.

MacIntyre is right in that virtues (and vices) are indeed more likely to be produced, learned and sustained in small-scale, face-to-face contexts where there may be a greater degree of proximity and shared understanding about the good. These may be local, vocational, religious, immigrant or other communities, voluntary organisations in civil society, trade unions, and so on. However, the small community is not the only type of community in which a substantive morality of virtues and practices can develop. MacIntyre does not say that only small face-to-face communities qualify as communities; he argues only that it is in this type of community that practices and virtues are more likely to flourish. This does not preclude us from looking at regions, nations or Europe as communities, or from exploring the possibility that virtues and practices actually can and do flourish within these other types of community.

Community comes in different degrees with respect to the ties that bind its constituents: ties may be looser in some cases and stronger in others. It also comes in at different levels – subnational, national and global (Mason 2000: 17–41); we might here add European. The ties of interest to us in this case are the moral ties, the shared conception of the good that involves particular virtues emerging from the community's practices. Supranational communities with looser moral ties are therefore no less communities than local communities that are more tightly knit from the moral point of view. Looser ties may develop into closer ties over time within a community; in other words, communities must not be taken as given – they evolve. There is a sense in which communities are always in-the-making. For the past fifty years we have been witnessing the emergence and evolution of a community that is the product of the voluntary coming together of several national communities, the European community. Constructivist approaches to international relations and the EU have provided useful insights about how community (or communities) can evolve beyond states through processes of communication, learning and deliberation (Linklater 1998; Eriksen and Fossum 2000; Shapcott 2001; Christiansen et al. 2001; Herrman et al. 2004; Adler 2005).

Furthermore, communities great and small are always in a state of internal moral evolution (MacIntyre 1988: 354–5). Within living communities, as within living practices, there is a continuous debate and joint enquiry about the good and what it entails. Such enquiry is essential to the pursuit of excellence and averts the moral and political sclerosis of communities. Moral enquiry is fed by internal or external stimuli or by internal contradictions. The evolving European community is receptive to internal moral stimuli coming from local and national communities, as well as external stimuli coming from other communities at different levels. By and large the European community is drawing on the practices and virtues of several communities that are internal and external with respect to it, and it can be shown to involve loose, gradual and voluntary convergence towards certain core features of one conception of the good. Clearly this conception of the good cannot be as comprehensive as it may be in small local communities (Etzioni 2007).

Small communities in Europe are not closed off from the rest of the world; they are indeed receivers of market values from national states, the EU and beyond, but they are also receivers of other external stimuli from the same source (or sources) that may enrich and renew their virtues and practices. Moreover, they are transmitters. Virtues may be produced, learned and cultivated at the small scale, but they may also be uploaded to the national and EU levels. There are some indications, when it comes to virtues and practices in the EU, that 'practice transfer' may be leading to 'virtue transfer'.

To take a few examples: the European Social Model and social partnership are made up of practices and accompanying virtues from certain member states and several local communities, in particular from central and northwest Europe. Transparency and its related virtues, originating in Scandinavian countries and communities, have come to influence the practices of the EU bureaucracy and political personnel. We saw analytically in the first chapter how French administrative virtues and practices determined the type of leadership and esprit de corps of the European Commission.

In turn, EU practices and virtues download back to the national and the local communities, providing external stimuli for internal debate and potential change. Local and national communities respond to such stimuli with diverse timing and in diverse ways. Stronger environmental norms and practices that have been transposed to the national and local levels and the practices to which they have given rise may have also been decisive for virtues related to the protection and respect for the environment that might otherwise not have developed in southern and eastern European nations and local communities. The same is true for practices embedded in EU equal opportunities policies, which may be encouraging the development of virtues related to the co-operative relations of the emerging dual-breadwinner family model in southern European communities. Clearly then, virtues and practices can and do develop in communities other than small-scale local communities, in this case both at the national level and in the EU.

A few clarifications are due at this point regarding certain aspects of the process of the evolution of communities that may lead to stronger moral ties. The Western experience of national community-building involved a process whereby a strong and centralised state apparatus, guided by a united and determined political elite and buttressed by an intellectual elite, forcibly constructed community through educational and cultural policies, with mass media playing a significant role in identity formation. The centre selectively evoked some of the possible elements of history, traditions, ideological trends and values to create and instil a common identity upon the population. That identity certainly involved participation in common national practices and the construction and propagation of 'national' virtues. This is a top-down and statist view of the formation and evolution of moral community.

Some scholars have engaged in comparisons of European nation-building with the process of community building in Europe and have concluded that there is not a great deal of difference between the two, as European identity formation is equally top-down and elite-driven (Costa 2004). The view taken here is different. The process of community formation (as opposed to the process of economic integration) in the EU cannot be top-down as there is no centralised 'state' that could plan a strategy in this direction, cultural and educational policies are firmly in the hands of national states, albeit loosely co-ordinated at European level, and there is no cohesive political or intellectual elite that could bring such a process forward or a coherent moral project behind which such an elite might mobilise. The building of moral community in the EU is in part taking place from the bottom up, and it does not necessarily mean annihilating – but may mean englobing and drawing on – the moralities of smaller communities.

These arguments show that Europe can be understood as a community-in-the-making, in which virtues and practices can flourish. In normative terms they provide support to the claim for respect for diversity within and across national states and within the EU. National states and the EU would do well to allow for and support the autonomy of small-scale communities which form the backbone of morality understood in terms of virtue and to provide content for the good because the communities they claim to represent benefit and flourish when virtues are produced and then uploaded.

Furthermore, local as well as national communities, which run the risk of being stagnant, closed and biased without internal and external stimuli, can benefit but should be allowed leeway in the way they receive and elaborate the new EU practices and related virtues, when these are downloaded, so that their own internal evolution is not disrupted. The greater the interaction between levels, the greater the possibility that the EU will continue to develop as a moral community and the greater the possibility that national and local communities will continue to be living communities.

Not only is it appropriate to apply the communitarian account of legitimacy to the EU, but it arguably provides insights that neither liberal egalitarian approaches nor neo-republican approaches can bring into the picture. Appealing to moral community in Europe as understood in terms of virtues and practices can explain why the behaviour of European Commissioners in the 1999 resignation was not simply judged to break the rules or to bear undesirable consequences but was considered bad in itself and deemed to discredit Commission practices as a whole. It may also elucidate the potential basis of citizen allegiance with the EU, since this is a question that neither liberal egalitarians nor neo-republicans can easily answer.

The virtue-based account does not require ethnic, cultural or other pre-political and pre-moral ties as prerequisites to legitimacy. Liberal egalitarian 'thin' attachments are too weak to command allegiance while strong active citizenship constitutive of and constituting political community may be too optimistic a scenario unless common moral understandings expressed as virtues within practices, however minimal, are built up in parallel across Europe. It may well be that convergence towards elements of a common morality is the necessary accompaniment of the discursive processes of political community formation envisaged by neo-republicans.

Other advocates of this view, such as Amitai Etzioni, speak not of virtues and participation in common practices as constitutive of moral community but of common values and affective ties. He argues that those can be built at the European level through public 'moral dialogues' – that is, 'public discussions that engage values rather than merely interests or wants', such as the desirability of the death penalty or the legalisation of gay marriages (Etzioni 2007). The advantage of understanding moral community in terms of virtues and practices rather than values is that values may be argued to be closely linked to established beliefs that are in turn related to comprehensive religious or cultural doctrines and are difficult to stand back from or reconsider. Practices and virtues on the other hand can be transferred, are learned through participation and are evaluated according to the extent to which internal goods are achieved and excellence promoted within practices.

The internal scrutiny of practices

The fact that in the communitarian account of legitimacy the criteria for evaluating a practice are to be drawn from within that practice has been argued to be problematic. It has been argued that the account does not allow for moral evaluation of the practice from an external point of view, as do both deontological and consequentialist approaches. This means that a practice of governance, for example, could function well in its own terms, and therefore be legitimate, but at the same time be totalitarian, aggressive or harmful towards third parties. Likewise, it could be legitimate but still be racist or sexist (Frazer and Lacey 1994). The objection could therefore be raised that the communitarian account would not constitute an adequate theory for assessing the legitimacy of governance because it comes up against the problem of 'evil practices'.

Against these objections it may be sustained that, from the MacIntyrean perspective, the most appropriate viewpoint from which to assess the legitimacy of a practice is indeed internal, but only insofar as critical enquiry and evaluation of the practice form part of the practice itself.

The internal moral scrutiny of practices may be thought of as occurring through a two-step process: first, contradictions and conflicts between virtues and goods within practices arise internally as the practice's standards of excellence and ends evolve over time, or as a result of stimuli coming from outside the practice. The former might include conflicts arising from the ways in which the achievement of different goods dictate different courses of virtuous action, or conflicts arising from different interpretations of what particular virtues require in a given context. The latter might comprise virtue-laden practices embedded in communities that come into contact with other communities or other practices within the same community.

Second, certain sub-practices within the practice develop over time, and these provide regular opportunities to address conflicts that arise between virtues and goods, or to elaborate stimuli, thus facilitating critical evaluation of the practice. Within contemporary Western practices of governance, examples of such sub-practices are accountability, democratic elections, judicial review and wealth redistribution through taxation. In turn, each of these sub-practices requires for its own operation a particular set of virtues. For example, accountability requires the virtues of responsibility, redistribution requires the virtues of solidarity, and so on.

When these sub-practices fail to develop, or when they work badly, the effect is detrimental for the legitimacy of the practice for two reasons. First, the virtues associated with the particular sub-practice do not develop at all or die out, with the result that corresponding internal goods are no longer achieved. The legitimacy of the practice itself understood in communitarian terms is undermined. Second, the possibility of addressing conflicts between virtues and goods or of elaborating stimuli – and therefore the very possibility of evaluating whether the practice is legitimate or not – is weakened. In order to examine the legitimacy of a practice, we must therefore focus on the relationship between virtues and critical sub-practices and the operation of the sub-practices in question.

Legitimate governance and political responsibility

According to the communitarian account developed here, the legitimacy of the practice of governance may be argued to involve various conceptions (for example, responsible, democratic, just, efficient or impartial), each characterised by a particular set of virtues, which enable the achievement of a particular good (or set of goods) internal to the practice. Responsible governance would thus be characterised by the virtues of responsibility that enable the achievement of the goods of order, democratic governance by the virtues of self-rule that enable the achievement of the good of collective autonomy, and so on. Each conception of legitimate governance is also associated with at least one sub-practice of internal scrutiny (responsible governance with accountability, democratic governance with elections, egalitarian governance with redistribution, and so forth).

The responsible conception of legitimate governance may then be associated with practising the virtues of responsibility, which in the next section will be argued to be reliability, coherence, trustworthiness and prudence. The internal goods that the virtues of responsibility are meant to enable the achievement of are order, stability, predictability. The core sub-practice that can be associated with responsible governance is accountability, whose necessary but not sufficient preconditions are openness and identifiability, as will be shown in the final section.

Different conceptions of legitimacy within the communitarian account (involving responsible, democratic, just, impartial, or egalitarian governance) might lead a virtuous agent to different conclusions about how to act. A virtuous member of the European Convention who represented a national government could, for example, be torn between exercising the virtues of responsibility (by being a reliable and trustworthy partner to their peers), those of impartiality (by tending to consider all relevant interests) and those of democracy (by tending to support their partial views and interests while being ready to accept being on the losing side) when required to take a position on issues that could turn out to be sensitive at home. Different internal goods, the achievement of which is enabled by particular virtues, may be at odds. Order arguably took precedence over justice in the choice of economic policy that was written into EMU (with the 'stability culture' pitted against welfare spending).

A series of questions arise at this point. When conflicts do arise, how are they to be dealt with? Should some goods internal to the practice of exercising political authority (i.e. order) always be preferred to others (i.e. equality or justice)? Ought some virtues (i.e. responsibility) always to be exercised before others (i.e. the democratic virtues or those of solidarity) as a consequence? And are therefore some sub-practices (i.e. accountability) always to take priority over others (i.e. democratic elections or redistributive practices) when decisions are taken on institutional arrangements?

Liberal egalitarian accounts deal with conflicts between principles and goods through a weighing procedure, which may for example take the form of the Rawlsian 'reflective equilibrium'. Neo-republican accounts imply a hierarchy of goods on top of which stands non-domination and a political process through which the specific orderings of the (common) goods to be achieved is formulated.

The communitarian account set out here is clearly contextual. One can only weigh the goods, the virtues and the sub-practices that are to assume priority in the contexts of particular instances of policy choice and policy-making, periods of institutional or constitutional reform or radical change, crises and failures, or successful completion of political projects that take place in particular communities at particular times. It follows that in particular communities (for example the EU) at different times (for instance the post-war period as opposed to the late twentieth century), achieving certain goods will justifiably take priority over achieving others (order versus justice), some virtues will be called for more than others (virtues of responsibility versus those of democracy) and some sub-practices will be assigned primacy over others, and this will become evident in institutional choice (efficiency practices over democratic elections, accountability or redistribution). The choices made and the judgements exercised during the European Convention, or indeed throughout the post-Maastricht constitutional debate, can be examined in this light from the point of view of legitimacy.

Political responsibility as a set of virtues

Political responsibility as a requirement upon political agency can be understood as a set of political virtues. We often speak of responsible citizens, responsible politicians, responsible policies proposed by a political party, or governments that have behaved responsibly. Weber speaks, in this same sense, of the 'ethics of responsibility' (Weber 1978: 218). In such cases, we use the term 'political responsibility' as a term of praise and, in response to the question of what it is that makes a politician or government, etc, responsible, we would give a list of the qualities of character, traits of excellence or virtues that are particular to the agents of such activity. It might be asked what binds the political virtues of responsibility together as a category. The virtues that fall under that heading portray a wise, sober and rational agent that never acts spontaneously before weighing the facts and deciding what is the right course of action (Pennock 1979: 268). Such an agent always does things with the right kind of detachment and for good reason, is absolutely steady and firm and is therefore predictable – a shield against uncertainty and arbitrariness. If this agent were a person and this person were in our circle of friends, we would certainly respect them, and perhaps go to them for advice, but we might find them tedious at times. On the other hand, if this agent were a person in a political role or were a government, we would praise them (or it) for being responsible.

The political virtues of responsibility are those of reliability, trustworthiness consistency and prudence. In the terms we have set out, if they are indeed political virtues, they would have to be qualities that enable the achievement of the goods internal to governance – that is, predictability, order and stability. It becomes clear, after examination of each one in turn, that they do.

Reliability

A responsible person, says Lucas,

> is one who can be left in charge, who can be relied on to cope, who will not slope off, leaving the job undone, or switch off, leaving the business unattended to. So long as a responsible person is responsible, you can sleep easy, knowing that no extra vigilance on your part is called for, and that he will see to it that all goes well. 'Responsible' in this sense is an adjective, denoting a quality of character and mind, not a position within a web of dialectical obligation ... It is a term of high commendation, though from an external point of view. We want to have responsible people about in positions of authority, performing their duties reliably and well. (Lucas 1993: 11)

A responsible political agent, then, is one who is reliable, who will get the job done, voluntarily and on their own initiative, even when they are not being directed, supervised or coerced. We value reliability because we conduct our lives in conditions of uncertainty; in the absence of a mechanism of co-ordination before the future, none of us individually has the means to deal with uncertainty effectively. Governance provides such a mechanism, and the political agency involved in governance is what makes it operative. The initiative of dealing with uncertainty is expected from that political agency which is involved in governance. Dealing with uncertainty means being able to foresee (to a reasonable extent) the alternatives and to prepare for them on the behalf of the collectivity. To deal with uncertainty we need to rely on the agents of governance. To put it another way, we need reliable agents involved in governance. We need to be confident that this function will be performed, regardless of how well we can control whether it is being performed or not, because we need to be confident that someone is actually taking the initiative and thinking ahead. Being reliable is taking the initiative whether or not it is subject to control. Reliability enables the achievement of predictability because it would not be possible to tackle uncertainty if all (or most) political agents were unreliable in the context of governance.

Trustworthiness

A reliable agent of governance is one that can be trusted to do things that we would not like to leave to chance. A political agent truly worthy of trust is not merely one that can be trusted to 'do the job' in absence of a better alternative. We trust this agent because we have good reason to do so (Raz 1994: 352–3). Good reason is proof given through a series of actions. We may consider that a single action was a responsible one, but when we attribute the character trait 'responsible' to an agent, we have in mind a sequence of actions. The more this sequence, or pattern of behaviour, reveals itself, the more the agent can be characterised as 'responsible', the more they become trustworthy, and the better we can predict whether or not the agent will live up to the standards that they have accustomed us to.

Unlike reliability, trustworthiness enables the achievement of the predictability that political agents require of each other and of government with respect to what is already known and agreed upon, not with respect to how and how well they deal with what is not yet known but only speculated upon. Furthermore, trustworthiness enables the implicit agreement, or common understanding, that constitutes a stable environment of interaction among political agents (Dunn 1990: 34). Without trustworthy political agents we would not be able to count on anyone keeping to their side of the social and communicative agreement. Order and stability, and therefore co-operation and co-ordination, would not be possible, because this agreement would not be adhered to and so would have no force or validity. Trustworthiness is thus a quality of political agents that enables predictability, order and stability in the context of governance.

Consistency

A responsible political agent is a consistent agent. They follow a course of action that is part of a plan with steps that lead to the end target. Sometimes, as a response to changing political circumstances and priorities, there may be good reason to break with what has been done in the past; this will mean a show of incoherence unless justification is provided. Lack of coherence without justification is taken as an indication of a lack of responsibility.

Coherence in governance is valued because it assures the continuity of long-term projects that need their time to become effective. In political agents involved in governance, coherence is valued because it demonstrates that they are capable of carrying out such projects, it shows that they do not continually change their minds about important and less important things, and it indicates that they are themselves sufficiently convinced about what they are doing. Coherence here concerns a show of consistency with respect to publicly expressed positions across a temporal range as well as between positions held in public and their corresponding actions – the consistency of words and deeds. Coherence enables the achievement of a certain degree of stability, which is necessary for long-term projects. It also enables order by structuring expectations in the long term. In other words, consistency allows us to anticipate the next steps, to programme and to plan.

Prudence

The responsible political agent, or responsible government, is primarily a prudent one. Prudent agents take the long-term rather than the short-term view and are, for this reason, cautious about the consequences of the measures and the positions that they take in public. To be prudent is to include in one's plans what can reasonably be foreseen and to work out in a specific way what steps must be taken. This requires 'not merely that one will act with regard for the consequences, but that one will evaluate and weigh the consequences properly' (Haydon 1978: 52). According to Aristotle, 'it is the mark of the prudent person to have deliberated well' (*NE*: 1142b31).

Prudence is concerned both with universals and with particulars, it needs both theoretical and practical knowledge, and it is acquired not only through knowledge but also, and mainly, through experience (*NE*: 1141a19–2a15).

In effect, prudence is the understanding that the political agent occupying a role in government has of what can be brought about with the means and resources at their disposal, to what extent it can be brought about and which complications might ensue. Government is endowed with the means to the realisation of common ends; these means are on one hand limited and on the other hand tremendously powerful in their possible effects. The political virtue of prudence allows for the correct use of means in order for the ends to be reached in the best way possible. By leading in this direction, prudence enables order in a very basic sense: if political agents are imprudent, all can be lost. Internal order collapses under the weight of inefficiency and conflict; external threats become stronger as internal order becomes weaker.

It is in these ways that the virtues of political responsibility enable the achievement of the goods of responsible governance – that is, predictability, order and stability.

Political responsibility as a property of institutions

In a Madisonian world, the institutions of governance would be designed to protect the system from the non-virtuous, because people can generally be expected to abuse power once it is in their grasp (Hamilton *et al.* [1788], 2000). In a Humean world, the institutions of governance would be designed for knaves – that is, with the presupposition that role occupants will act as knaves, even if people are not knaves (Hume 1742: 117–26). In a republican world, the institutions of governance would be designed to foster virtue, of which civically minded citizens, attached to institutions, are considered capable (Dagger 1997, Pettit 1997).

In the MacIntyrean world, institutions are necessary for the material sustenance of practices, which in turn provide the necessary context within which the virtues can flourish (MacIntyre 1981). Yet, institutional design is not enough to ensure that the virtues will be promoted: as argued above, much would also depend on the forging of moral community. Appropriate design can, however, encourage the development of virtuous agency within practices and guarantee that if, and insofar as, such agency is available, institutions will, in simple terms, reward the virtuous and punish the vicious. How, then, must the institutions of governance be set up if they are to sustain the practice of governance and the virtues of political responsibility?

Political responsibility is commonly understood to be a requirement imposed not only on political agency but also on the institutions of governance. It will be argued in this section that this second category refers to certain properties of the institutions of governance which ensure that the flourishing of the virtues of political responsibility is encouraged, their presence rewarded and their absence punished within the practice of governance.

Two questions will be addressed: in the context of the institutional make-up of governance, how are the 'signals' that responsible agency is appropriate issued? And what are the sanctions that can be provided by a system of governance if responsible agency is to be rewarded and irresponsibility punished? Signals cannot be one-off events and sanctions must be expected. Moreover, they must – in some way – involve (or be recognised by) all the political agents operating in the context of the general practice of governance, whatever their political role, because the logic of appropriateness that we assume to be the motivational force of agents *vis à vis* institutions requires that notions of what is appropriate are shared notions. What comes to mind first is the practice of accountability. Accountability must be supported by governance institutions if the virtues of responsibility are to be sustained and the goods of governance produced.

Accountability is periodic, publicly practised and backed by sanctions. It is meant to signal the desirability of the full set of the virtues of political responsibility and to make this signal effective by backing it with sanctions. The periodic nature of accountability is a call for consistency: at a certain point, political agents must account for their actions and show that what they said and did since the last time they were called to account are not miles apart; if they are, the political agent in question must try to defend this in terms that are publicly justifiable. The public nature of accountability is meant to encourage political agents to be prudent: if they must justify what they have said and done in public, then they must show that they have taken the overall view, that they have considered all the interests they were mandated to consider, and that they have not sacrificed the long term benefit of the community for short term benefits, although they have tried to reconcile the two. The sanction that accompanies accountability is meant (in principle) to reward the political agent who has been reliable and trustworthy. A political agent who is shown not to have acted when circumstances have called for action or a political agent who is shown not to have kept promises will be ousted from office, if practices of accountability are effective.

Accountability involves all political agents in the context of governance. There are many reasons for this. Firstly, it is not enough that there is one political agent (or several political agents) held to account and another political agent (or several other political agents) holding the former to account. Accountability is a public process in the context of which both parties are under scrutiny and where the actions and judgements of both are approved or disapproved of. Secondly, accountability is a process that could affect any political agent, by virtue of their being a political agent, that is, a potential or actual participant in political practices. Thirdly, the judgements made in the context of accountability make appeal to reasons, norms and virtues that are shared by all or recognised by all.

Accountability is effective when there are adequate checks upon the acts of political agents and an efficient forum through which positive and negative sanctions can be debated, justified and allocated before the public eye.

Accountability fails when politically responsible agency is not selected – that is, when responsible political agency is not rewarded or when irresponsible political agency is not punished. Such situations discourage political responsibility by giving out the signal – or lesson – that politically responsible agency is not considered valuable.

It may be asked what it takes for accountability to be possible in the first place. One way is to ensure that everyone within the institutional structure knows who is responsible for what. What will here be termed identifiability is in place when the role structure is clear, simple and stable and when the norms of adhering to one's role-related tasks and taking responsibility for them are binding. Another is for the institutional structure to ensure that political agents are equipped with enough information and the required capacity for judgement that they are able to participate in the process of accountability. This is the requirement of openness. Openness is effective when it is appropriately delimited as well as when the system of governance is transparent.

Accountability, identifiability and openness may be described as the requirements that the principle of political responsibility places upon the institutions of governance. If these requirements are met in the institutions of governance then the failure of political responsibility is likely to be due to the weakness of moral community, which, as argued above, is the necessary background against which the virtues in general and those of responsibility in particular are produced and cultivated. If on the contrary there is a solid community, or one in the making, but these institutional properties are non-existent, then observed failures of political responsibility may well be due to institutional design.

In the context of the EU, both weakness of the ties of moral community and faulty institutional design seem to be behind the failures of political responsibility. The development of community is likely to be a slow and cumbersome process, which cannot and ought not to be 'commanded', while institutional design for the last twenty years has been, and continues to be, a top concern for the Union's political and economic elites and, increasingly, for citizens. In view of this, the next three chapters will focus on the institutional requirements of political responsibility in the EU and will attempt to identify that aspect of the 'responsibility deficit' which is due to institutional design and to evaluate the extent to which recent changes are ameliorating or further worsening the situation.

Conclusion

The main task of this chapter has been to put forward a notion of political responsibility and to show why political responsibility is desirable in the context of governance. It was shown that political responsibility as a requirement upon agency and as a requirement upon institutions, represent two sides of the same coin, rather being unrelated or only loosely related.

The virtues of political responsibility (reliability, coherence, trustworthiness and prudence) are desirable in the context of governance, both in themselves and because they enable the achievement of the goods internal to governance (predictability, order and stability). The institutional aspects of political responsibility (accountability, identifiability and openness) are essential for the reproduction, or selection, of politically responsible agency – that is, political agency characterised by the virtues of political responsibility. Although they cannot fully guarantee the presence of politically virtuous agency in a system of governance, they can encourage its development and guarantee that, insofar as it manifests itself, it will be rewarded. Even if we cannot command politically responsible agency into existence, we can nevertheless design institutions that will encourage and select it; therefore, if we consider it worthwhile for a system of governance to be characterised by political responsibility, it is important that we assess its institutions in this light. It is important, in other words, to examine whether accountability, identifiability and openness exist in the institutions of EU governance, to see whether they are effective and to seek alternative institutional solutions that will support them if they are not.

3

Accountability

Introduction

This chapter will examine accountability as a sub-practice of EU governance. It will first distinguish between political and other forms of accountability, then try to spell out the basic rationale behind political accountability and examine what we do – and do not do – when we hold someone to account. Next, it will be shown that in order for accountability to be effective, the institutional structure in a system of governance must meet two requirements: what we will call 'check' and 'forum'. In the second part of the chapter we will examine the extent to which the requirements of accountability are being met in the EU, taking into account recent developments in the Constitutional Treaty and the Lisbon Treaty.

Political and other forms of accountability

To be accountable to someone for something is to be under the obligation to give an account to a certain agent that is assigned to receive this account. It consists in answering questions about one's actions regarding a particular task by producing a coherent set of explanations and justifications. Accountability is the institutionalised practice that being accountable gives rise to.

The practice of accountability can be encountered in the spheres of inter-personal morality, law and elsewhere. The specifically political practice of accountability has certain particularities that distinguish it from the practices of accountability in other spheres of human activity. In opposition to moral accountability, where one is accountable only in exceptional cases when one has done something morally wrong, political accountability is formally institutionalised, regularly enacted and public. It may include positive as well as negative assessment. Furthermore, moral accountability is in principle owed to every moral agent, whereas political responsibility is owed to specifically designated political agents. In the former there is no one in an a priori privileged position to hold others accountable, whereas the latter is rooted in a fixed structure of political roles, among which political accountability is organised. Within this structure, occupants of political roles know with respect to their roles to whom they are accountable. By contrast, legal accountability is a practice the purpose of which is to pass legal sanction on legal persons who are in breach of legal obligations. It is a practice that takes place within fixed requirements specified by the law, the breach of which incurs punishment from an impartial standpoint. The relationship of political accountability to political sanction is not quite so straightforward, owing to the nature and aims of political sanction as well as to the effect that its public dimension has on the motivation of political agents.

What we do not do when we hold a political agent to account

Thomas Nagel uses the terms 'judge' and 'defendant' to illustrate the interpersonal case of moral accountability in the *View from Nowhere*. He claims that when we hold someone to account we are attempting to occupy their position in terms of reasons and options for the actions they have performed (Nagel 1986: 120–4). Although this may be the case in moral accountability, it is not so in political accountability. This is because in politics, we always hold (and often are obliged to hold) someone to account from within a particular political role (in the case of institutional accountability) or a particular political partisan position (in the case of political opposition). Someone's political role or political partisan position is the 'view' from which they hold another to account. This means two things: firstly, the 'view' of the 'judge' will always be different from the that of the 'defendant', given their different political role or partisan position; secondly, the view of the 'judge' will be different from that of the real judge, whose view is supposed to be an impartial one. The metaphor of 'judge' and 'defendant' does not, in fact, hold in politics, where there is no such position as the privileged one of a real judge. 'Judge' and 'defendant' are both parts of a practice whose purpose is to set and enforce the standards of what is politically 'right' and what is politically 'wrong'. This is why, from the practice of political accountability, positive as well as negative judgements can result. According to Grey, this is in itself 'a political act carried out in a political context':

> assertions about blame, damage and responsibility can never be established authoritatively by dispassionate, objective analysis. Disastrous events are thus socially and politically constructed, rather than 'discovered' by scientific evaluation. (Grey 1998: 9)

We must keep in mind, however, that this process does not take place arbitrarily: it always operates within a structure of political institutions and takes into account a specific system of political roles. It is true that judges and journalists have played 'judge' at exceptional occasions when a democratic political system as a whole was in crisis, but these situations rightly remain exceptional.

Another thing that we do not do when we hold someone politically accountable is to blame them without due reflection. What we do when we hold others to account has been the subject of a debate which has evolved around the notion of 'reactive attitudes', put forward by Strawson. Strawson claims that there is an emotional, non-cognitive level – that of the reactive attitudes, such as resentment, gratitude, forgiveness, indignation, and so on – at which we operate in our interpersonal relationships (Strawson 1968: 74–7). He suggests that to treat others as morally accountable is to be disposed to respond to them with the reactive attitudes. Moral praise and blame (the basis of moral sanction) can be interpreted to express such reactive attitudes rather than being connected with moral reasons (Strawson 1968: 77–96). This approach has been viewed favourably as taking into account certain elements that 'behaviouralist' approaches do not take into account (Wallace 1996: 55).

However, this approach has been criticised for its non-cognitivism: for Scanlon, one of the things we do when we make moral judgements is indeed to express attitudes, but it is not the essential thing; it is quite possible to make a moral judgement without expressing any particular attitude. The force of moral blame, according to Scanlon, can be accounted for in a different way: by the fact that people care about the justifiability of their actions to others (Scanlon 1988: 165–72). Judgements of moral blame assert that what the agent did was not in accordance with what others motivated to reach agreement would not reasonably reject (Scanlon 1982: 116–17).

Wallace contends that there is an attitudinal difference between moral blame and criticism, which is that 'moral blame has a quality of opprobrium that is lacking in criticism of beliefs or opinions ... It is one thing to criticise a philosopher's views about causation and quite another thing to blame the philosopher for supporting racist or sexist hiring practices' (Wallace 1996: 80–1). This could turn out to be a questionable distinction; is the cognitive element not there when we blame the philosopher for their political position? And is it not true that criticism can become bitterly 'emotional'?

It may well be that Strawson's reactive attitudes are – at least partly – relevant to the understanding of moral accountability, but Scanlon is closer to the motivation of political agents in the context of political accountability, where the publicity of the practice and the regularity of the demand for justification structure the practice differently in terms of the attitudes of the political agent that holds another to account. If there are reactive attitudes in politics, the practice of political accountability is meant to contain them within the framework of attributing blame to the right place for the right reasons. It is when political accountability fails that we have outbreaks of unreflective blame.

What we do when we hold a political agent to account

When we hold someone politically accountable, we assess their actions as well as their conduct – we evaluate both an act and an actor. Insofar as we assess actions, we think of the consequences of these actions, and it is in the light of these consequences that the assessment takes place. Insofar as we assess conduct, we take under consideration the agent's intentions and their motivation to act in one particular way rather than another. It is certainly the case that someone's actions reflect on their conduct and characterise it. But there is a temporal dimension to this. Certainly, a one-off bad or mistaken act cannot influence our assessment of an agent's conduct in the same way that a series of such acts could. An agent's conduct is assessed over a period of time, whereas an agent's act is assessed at a certain point in time. Conversely, an act may acquire different values in different contexts, where the assessment of the conduct of an agent may remain the same across different contexts. The same act may cause different consequences in different contexts and therefore be evaluated differently. To hold someone to account requires two separate assessments: that of an act against the background of a certain political context and that of an agent's conduct against the background of a certain temporal length.

There are various reasons why we hold someone to account. Firstly, because we have certain views about how political agents ought to go about their tasks and expect them to uphold certain standards of political conduct. We want to be able to hold the agents to these expectations and to sanction them when they fail to act accordingly. This is a backward-looking account: sanction is meant to punish or reward an agent for his or her acts, reconfirming and reinforcing the standards held by a political community in its operation (Markovits and Silverstein 1988: 2–4). Lucas calls this aim of sanction 'vindicative' (Lucas 1993: 92–3). Secondly, we hold someone to account because we want to sanction their political acts. According to a forward-looking, consequentialist account, the infliction of sanction for a certain act is aimed at the augmentation of overall social utility, which will come about if certain political agents are made an example of, negatively or positively. This 'exemplary' aim of sanction underlies the mechanism of political accountability. In other words, in the first case, we are more concerned about the agent: we want to bring the agent in line with the approved standards of political conduct In the second case, we are more concerned about the act that the agent has done and we want to control the implications that it might have in terms of its becoming a precedent or an example. (Smiley 1992: 239; March and Olsen 1995: 154).

Do we have to make a choice between the two accounts? In other words, are the two accounts incompatible? The answer is no – at least, not if we look carefully at what constitutes political sanction. Punishments and rewards in politics are of a certain kind. To remove someone from political office is not like sacking them from their job; it need not result in their losing the respect of their friends and family or the loss of freedom that sending them to jail would inflict on them. Removal from political office could well be accompanied by these kinds of sanction, but it is not necessarily so. On the reward side, being elected or assigned to a position of high political power is nothing like being paid a large sum of money or like being given a warm welcome at the airport by a large group of friends. But sanctions are not exclusively reserved for extremes: it is not only when political agents are removed from office that they are sanctioned. The opposition sanctions the government on a regular basis; the electorate sanctions governments by turning down or embracing its policies; and political parties gain in strength or disappear from the political map.

Political sanction is, in the case of punishment, extremely severe – or, in the case of reward, extremely elevating – because of its public dimension (Bovens 1998: 39–40). It is based on a twofold assessment of the suitability of a political agent. Firstly, it assesses their suitability for the office that they hold; secondly, it goes deeper to touch on their very status as a political agent. Suitability becomes the focus of public attention: in the first case, positive or negative sanction is directed at what makes an agent suitable to play a certain part in the making of decisions that determine the common fate; in the second case it goes to the very heart of what makes that agent fit to be a member of a political community.

This is exactly the point where the 'vindicative' aim of accountability meets the 'exemplary' one. That the sanctioning of particular political agents in politics takes place publicly gives political sanction a dimension of exemplifying, which in principle is meant to work towards reinforcing the desirable standards of political conduct. The problem with acknowledging the forward-looking account on its own is that it could justify the sanctioning of political agents for exemplary purposes even if they were not blameworthy, only to make an example of an act. The problem with the backward-looking account on its own is that it would understate the importance of the public function of political sanction, which goes beyond an individual's particular faults to encompass the community's political *modus vivendi* (Wallace 1996: 57, 61).

To sum up what has been said so far about political accountability from the point of view of the one holding another to account: when we hold one to account we assess both the agent and the act, when we sanction someone as a result of having held them to account, our reasons for doing so are both our will to keep the conduct of political agents in line with what the political community considers appropriate and our wish to make an exemplary assessment of certain kinds of acts for future reference. This is the basic rationale in the practice of accountability. In what follows, it will be argued that if accountability is to be possible, there are certain requirements that the institutions of any system of governance must meet.

Check and forum

If accountability is meant to ensure that political agents are accountable for their *acts*, it is imperative that institutions make it possible to check certain acts systematically. In other words, a system of governance must incorporate a system of positive and negative sanctions, so that when a certain act has been performed it is automatically sanctioned, or so that precautionary measures to stop a certain act from taking place are institutionalised. What is more important here is that an act has taken place, or can be expected to take place; not who it was that performed it, or can be expected to perform it. It is the act that must be sanctioned, not the agent. Such a system of sanctions can take many forms: periodical public account-giving, parliamentary motions of censure, 'disciplinary' measures, special courts, periodical and exceptional checks, selection and hiring procedures, votes of investiture, veto points, and so on.

On the other hand, if accountability is meant to ensure that political *agents* are accountable for their acts, institutions must be set up in such a way that political agents can be effectively rewarded or punished publicly. In other words, accountability requires a forum, in the context of which punishments and rewards can be debated, justified and allocated before the public eye. The target of sanction here is the political agent and their conduct across a temporal length, not the individual acts that they have performed or can be expected to perform. The function of forum can be and is used in the context of elections and electoral campaigns, debates in parliamentary assemblies and committees, and in the media, referenda and so forth. Being punished before the public eye could mean that a role occupant loses their position or office and is replaced by another; it could mean that they are demoted to a position of lesser responsibility; or it could simply mean that they are publicly rebuked. Accordingly, being rewarded might entail being assigned a prestigious task, being promoted to a better position, or simply becoming the object of favourable public recognition and praise.

Check and forum are the two requirements of accountability that the institutions in a system of governance must meet. It is important that both requirements are met, because each on its own will not suffice if account-ability is to be made possible from the institutional side. With check on its own, accountability can degenerate into a closed enterprise for a principal and an agent, or for the expert few, without any reference to the standards that political activity should uphold; from this state of affairs, there are no 'lessons' to be learned. If there is just the forum without effective checks, accountability can be reduced to a dangerous witch-hunt, destructive for pub-lic life and public trust. This double requirement of check and forum is not acknowledged by most contemporary approaches to accountability, which are generally prone to give primacy to the check (or 'control') requirement, which they consider sufficient, and to neglect the forum requirement.

According to the dominant principal–agent approach, a principal delegates to an agent specific tasks that the principal may be unable or unwilling to perform. Agency problems exist when there is a discrepancy between the interests and preferences of the agent and those of the prin-cipal and when the agent cannot be effectively monitored by the principal (Kiewet and McCubbins 1991: 24–5). This is why the principal establishes certain safeguards to guarantee the agent's conformity to the agent's inter-ests or preferences (Bergman 2000: 3). Accountability, according to certain representatives of this approach, may refer to a process of control, or it may refer to a type of outcome. A process of control may not yield the outcome desired by the agent, while a desired outcome may come about not because there was a process of control but because the agent shares the goals of the principal and pursues them in any case. The outcome is argued to be more important in the discussion of accountability (Lupia 2000:18–19). Nevertheless, whether accountability is to be understood as a process of control or as the conformity of the outcome to the dictates of the principal, it is still control that is understood as the principal function of accountability (Pollack 2002); it is all about whether and how a principal can control an agent as to the specific tasks that the latter is supposed to perform. The forum requirement is not considered at all; in fact, what matters is the isolated relationship between a principal and an agent for specific acts and not the agent's acting in accordance with particular standards of political conduct.

Another example can be given by the trend of 'contracting out' in public administration, or, as it is called, the 'new public management'. In the 1980s and 1990s, and more so in the English-speaking world, the trend in public administration has been the establishment of contractual-type relationships between the government and private agencies, as well as between the government and its own departments, reorganised as semi-independent agencies, with a considerable degree of delegation of responsibility, in order to implement (often, not only implement but plan and evaluate as well) public business (Pollitt and Bouckaert 2000). This move has largely been justified not only on grounds of efficiency in the implementation of policy and in the workings of the public sector in general but also on grounds of promoting responsibility. Although it is said that the relevant political authority remains ultimately accountable for the outcomes, serious accountability gaps are known to have resulted in two areas. The first is where, on one hand, the government cannot effectively control the implementation of policy, while on the other hand, agencies can escape scrutiny or pass the buck to the government (Barker 1998: 1–23). The second is where the government passes the buck to agencies in order to avoid political responsibility (Harlow 2002: 22). This criticism of 'new public management' again focuses on control; and again, what is not discussed is that in the case where something goes wrong there are no lessons to be learned, because control may be exercised in a closed context and it is more likely to be exercised from a technical rather than a public–political point of view, accessible to most citizens.

By losing its function as forum, accountability becomes an internal process of control and is interpreted to refer to the evaluation of an outcome that any agent could have produced. The agent, according to these approaches, is not important, but the outcomes that they bring about are important. However, the agency problem is not (or at least not only) the fact that the principal and the agent do not share the same interests and preferences; nor is it that the agent did not do exactly what the principal wanted. The problem is (or it is also) that they may not share the same standards of political conduct. Furthermore, under conditions of complexity, if accountability is reduced to check, it becomes easy to underplay its significance altogether and to argue (as does Majone, for example) that, through independence, control can be exercised more effectively.

Majone argues that independent regulatory agencies have been an answer to the obvious 'mismatch between the increasingly specialised functions of government and the administrative instruments at its disposal' (Majone 1994: 5). The need for expertise and adjudication which are not to be conducted by governments or courts, as well as a divorce of certain issues from partisan politics in order to safeguard policy continuity and, above all, efficiency, are among the reasons that provide good justification for the rise of independent agencies (Majone 1994: 5). Of course, there are problems of accountability, whereby 'the crucial political issue is control' (Majone 1993: 6). According to Majone, independence is not a problem for accountability as control; rather, independence can complement accountability, provided that more flexible, multiple mechanisms of control are developed. These mechanisms of control do not have to emanate from a fixed centre, but they will work through their pluralism (Majone 1996a: 37–40). Independent agencies must be completely independent decisionally from political authorities. They, and everyone else, must, however, clearly know what outcome is to be produced and they must be subject to procedural requirements that can be easily controlled as to conformity by judicial review. They must give reasons for what they do and thus allow for control of their activities by judicial bodies, peers and citizens (Majone 1996b: 292–4). In this way, Majone argues, agencies would be no less accountable for their actions than politicians (Majone 1996b: 291); agencies can also 'protect citizens from bureaucratic arrogance and reticence, favour public participation (while the opportunity for consultation by means of public hearings is often denied to government departments) and focus public attention on controversial issues, thus enriching public debate' (Majone 1994: 22). Where European experience has shown us the opposite, it is because the relevant agencies were not independent enough (Majone 1994: 6–7).

The reason why the creation of independent agencies is argued to be desirable is that governments cannot and should not place complex technical matters, upon whose successful handling the general well-being depends, in the midst of the turbulence of party politics. Whether control for these issues can be successfully left to peers and professional codes and enforced by judges before the non specialist public eye is perhaps an empirical question; the same can be said for the assumption that independent agencies would be better motivated than governmental departments to be transparent about their operation and results. However, it is highly questionable that obtaining information about agency decision-making can be a substitute for the function of accountability as forum. If, through accountability, what is judged is not only the agent's actions but also their conduct, this judgement takes place against the yardstick of common political standards.

The standards to be reinforced in the case of independent agencies would be professional, scientific and juridical, and the ultimate goal would be that of microeconomic efficiency. Standards of political conduct would have no place in the life of independent agencies, which would, nevertheless, take crucial decisions about the general well-being and therefore, perform a role that is political (Føllesdal and Hix 2006).

In this section, it was argued that if accountability is to be effective, the institutions of governance must incorporate both check and forum. The neglect of one (the requirement of forum in most contemporary approaches to accountability) leaves us only partially aware of what accountability requires and can undermine the significance of accountability altogether.

When accountability fails

To be accountable is to be under the obligation to answer questions about one's acts. It is the case in modern, complex political systems that the political task follows a division of labour and the units of this division of labour are the multitude of interrelated and interdependent political roles that compose it. A political agent's obligation to answer is usually part of a system of political role-related obligation (Hart 1968: 212–14). The obligation to answer is circumscribed both as to its scope (that is, as to the things one is obliged to answer *for*) and as to its direction (that is, as to the person or entity one is obliged to answer *to*). Both of these limitations are set by the system of political roles within which the political agent in question operates. Accountability signals to role occupants that they are expected to do certain things that their role demands and to reach a certain level of role performance, below which the performance is considered inadequate and above which it may be considered arbitrary. In democracies, the obligation to provide an account for one's role-performance is usually part of one's role-related obligations. In such cases, when in breach of this obligation, one is subject to negative assessment not only for incompetence but also for arbitrariness. However, it is important to distinguish between incompetence and arbitrariness in political role performance. That one's role-performance was arbitrary does not provide much information about one's competence; one may have acted non-arbitrarily but nevertheless imprudently, inefficiently or recklessly; on the other hand, one may have done things that went beyond, or even against, the requirements of one's duties but nevertheless have acted with exceptional competence. Accountability encourages political agents to act in a way that is both non-arbitrary and competent with reference to the task that they are required to perform (Bovens 1998: 27).

To act in a non-arbitrary way – that is, not to go beyond one's role-related tasks – is to be reliable, trustworthy and coherent. A political agent who can be counted on to do what is required of them is a reliable political agent. A political agent who can be shown to actually do what they have to do across a temporal length is trustworthy; and one who is able to demonstrate that they have done what had to be done across a temporal length is coherent. To act in a competent way is to be efficient and prudent. A political agent who performed well as a result of taking the overall and the long-term view is what can simply be called prudent. In other words, by encouraging political agents to act with non-arbitrariness and competence, accountability encourages political agents to act in a politically responsible way.

The question to ask at this point is the following: encouraging politically responsible agency may well be what effective mechanisms of accountability do, but will simple encouragement suffice? Will agents make good on this expectation in the absence of sanction? In the context of political account-ability which is institutionalised, periodical and regular, the expectation that a political agent will be held to account and sanctioned is normally a factor that constrains and shapes all political action. Role occupants know that they will be expected to account for their role performance and they will normally act in a way that allows them to provide a defensible account for it. This expectation constrains agents to act in an effective and prudent way. Furthermore, being systematically held to account limits the range of acts one is willing and able to do. One will not normally do something that one cannot publicly explain and justify with some relation to the political task that lies within the scope of one's obligation to account for. The expectation of sanction constrains agents to act with reliability and coherence and to be trustworthy.

One example, which is central to democracies with respect to the way political sanction constrains and shapes political agency, is the electoral mechanism. Manin, Przeworski and Stokes examine two conceptions of the purpose of elections: they distinguish between the 'mandate' and the 'accountability' conceptions. In the first case, elections serve 'to select good policies or policy-bearing politicians' (Manin *et al.* 1999: 29). Voters make selections among political platforms put forward by parties, and the chosen platform becomes the 'mandate' that the government must implement. In the second case, 'elections serve to hold governments responsible for the results of their past actions. Because they anticipate the judgement of voters, governments are induced to choose policies that in their judgement will be positively evaluated by citizens at the time of the next election' (Manin *et al.* 1999: 29).

However, Fearon argues that voters think of elections as 'a declaration of who in the group most deserves the honour of political authority' or as a mechanism of distinguishing 'good types' of politician that are 'more inclined to act of their own accord in the public interest' (Fearon 1999: 58). This means that even if the breach of the obligation to answer questions does not carry political sanctions, the knowledge that one will be called to account publicly is enough to make one prepared to give an account *as if* one were to face political sanction (Bovens 1998: 28). This is because one can only attract praise or avoid blame through the device of political accountability. This is where it all comes out: how good an account one has for one's actions is important since this is a forum where one must prove one's role-performance and one's status as a political agent. If an agent is assessed for their acts within the specific context as well as for their conduct across a length of time, then any agent who wants to be praised for, or avoid being shamed for, their conduct will do their best to be judged positively for their acts over time by systematically providing an acceptable account of them. Acceptable accounts are exactly those accounts given by political agents who are in a position to show that they acted responsibly (Haydon 1978: 55); and political agents act responsibly not only through fear of being punished or publicly shamed but also in the hope that they will be publicly acknowledged and praised (Goodin 1992: 135).

If politically responsible agency is available but not 'selected' (that is, if the virtues of political responsibility are not called for and if politically responsible agents are not 'rewarded', while politically irresponsible political agents are not 'punished'), then we can say that accountability has failed. This can happen for many reasons: because accountability was not regularly expected or publicly enacted; because the institutional requirements of check and forum were not met; because, as will be seen in the next two chapters, identifiability and openness were not sufficient. In any case, failure to select politically responsible agency when it is available means failure of accountability.

Accountability in the EU

So far an attempt has been made to articulate the core rationale of the practice of (political) accountability, to point to the institutional requirements that a system of governance must meet if accountability is to be effective, and to explain what it means for accountability to fail. The EU system of governance can now be addressed, with a view to examining whether it meets the institutional requirements of accountability, taken to be check and forum.

Checks in the EU's institutions of governance

In the EU there is a dual executive: the Commission and the Council. It is often contested whether the Commission is a government or an administration (Page 1997: 147–8, Magnette 2003: 75–6), or a *sui generis* mixture of both (Peterson 1999: 47–8). We can say that the Commission has a political role, which stems from its right of initiative; it also has an administrative role, which comes from its role in administration, management and supervision of European policies (Nugent 2001: 326–7). The Council of Ministers on the other hand is both executive and, in some policy areas, legislator, together with the European Parliament (EP). In what concerns the Council's legislative role, there are different political majorities in Council and EP, which renders their relation comparable to that between two chambers in a federal system; their co-legislative role means that a mutual check between two bodies (EP and Council) is exercised, but this only holds where co-legislation is the deciding norm, which excludes Pillar 2 and also the governance of the Lisbon strategy, and generally where the norm is policy co-ordination rather than legislation. In terms of parliamentary check, it is weak overall: the EP checks the Commission, while national parliaments (NPs) individually check their respective governments in Council and collectively may check the Commission as a body.

With regard to the requirement for check, a number of mechanisms in the EU are designed to play this role, which correspond to different models of checks that can be distinguished in terms of comparative politics. At the EU level checks are to be thought of not in terms of straight lines of accountability, such as those that are to be found in parliamentary systems (although some elements of this kind are to be found as well), but at least partially as resembling the checks and balances mechanisms that are present in federal systems (Peterson 1997: 561). This is the case when we think of the two-chamber structure of the legislature (Council and EP), the significant role of the European Court of Justice, which can be argued to resemble a Constitutional Court, and the Union's particular dual executive structure involving the Council and the Commission. On the other hand, the relationship between the Commission and the EP brings the EU somewhat closer to a model of parliamentary accountability. More traditional accountability chains can also be discerned in the relationship between NPs and ministers in the Council. Finally a third model of checks is also implied by the Constitutional Treaty and carried forward with the Lisbon Treaty, with the provision for a long-term European Council President. While the new institution brings in elements of systems of checks that are to be found in presidential systems, the European Council President will not be elected indirectly through the Union's assemblies (Council and EP or NPs), or directly by the people, but chosen and appointed by the European Council and therefore checked only by the governments of the member states.

Checks on the European Commission

In what concerns its political role, the Commission is checked partly by the EP, since the Parliament hears both the president and the members of the Commission on their 'political programme' before voting them into office. The EP alone may vote the Commission out of office with a motion of censure. The investiture procedure takes place in two steps. First the Commission's president is appointed after a vote in the EP. The president then assembles a College, drawing candidate Commissioners from lists of three put forward by each national government. The EP then holds hearings with individual Commissioners and finally the College is voted into office as a group.

After the Santer Commission's resignation crisis, steps towards establishing more effective checks of the European Commission were taken with the Treaty of Nice and the European Constitutional Treaty. The Commission's president was given greater power over their choice of Commissioners and allocation of portfolios, and power was granted to them in reshuffling portfolios in the College and dismissing individual Commissioners (Treaty of Nice, 2001: Article 130). Neither the Constitutional Treaty nor the Lisbon Treaty assigned power to dismiss individual Commissioners to the EP. That power remains with the president of the Commission (Spence 2006: 42). The EP undertook a greater role in the appointment of the Commission through the institutionalisation of the hearings procedure. The Constitutional Treaty took this one step further by making the appointment of the Commission President dependent on the results of EP elections.

The EP's check that takes place through the investiture procedure is weakened by the fact that the president of the Commission and the individual Commissioners are nominated by the member states rather than from by the EP itself. As to the choice of president of the Commission, it is clearly a matter of intergovernmental bargaining between member states, which informally is expected to take several considerations into account. One set of considerations is related to the professional, administrative or political experience of prospective candidates, as well as to their status and personality. Another set of factors concerns the candidates' country of origin. Attempts are made to alternate between candidates from smaller and larger countries, as well as between candidates from countries in different regions of Europe – for example, north and south. Finally, the political affiliation of prospective candidates is important. In the past, the post was not monopolised by one political family but rather rotated among the major political families. More recently, it has been agreed that the choice of Commission president must reflect the outcome of the latest European elections and must therefore be drawn from the ranks of the political majority in the EP. Although the EP uses its vote to invest the president, and despite the fact that EU leaders are now obliged to take the outcome of the European elections into account, the choice of Commission president is clearly an intergovernmental choice, being the result of a broad agreement between the member states, negotiations for which are carried out at the highest level (Magnette 2003: 78–9).

With regard to the College, three nominations are put forward for each Commissioner from the respective member state, and the Commission's president may choose one from among the three candidates. Nonetheless, the hearings procedure developed by the EP has gained strength to such a degree that it can now force the president to change the name he has put forward for a particular portfolio. This became evident in the investiture of the 2004 Barroso College, when the EP forced President Barroso to withdraw the candidacy of Rocco Buttiglione by threatening to vote down the entire College. Before the vote, the EP had the numbers to back it, and it made this known to President Barroso, thus making the threat effective. Even if, however, the EP succeeds in forcing member states to withdraw a president candidate, or the president to withdraw a Commissioner candidate, it is not in a position to propose a new one.

Moreover, attempts to bring a motion of censure against the Commission have not so far been successful, even in the case of the Santer Commission crisis, where the vote of censure was lost, but the political opprobrium resulting from the Expert Group Report's findings forced the Commission to resign *en bloc*. In general terms, the majority needed in order for a motion of censure to pass is difficult to muster: there are divisions across party lines and members of the EP (MEPs) are vulnerable to pressures from their national centres. A motion of censure would be tantamount to a nuclear explosion for the Union.

During the Commission's term of office, where the EP co-legislates it is one of the two key players (along with the Council) that checks the proposing executive by feeding amendments into the Commission's proposals or rejecting proposals coming from the Commission's initiatives. Moreover, the Parliament grants annual discharge to the Commission for its management of the budget, while the Commission is also checked by virtue of the account that it is obliged to give at the EP when it presents its annual programme, when it is asked by MEPs to answer questions in the Plenary, or in standing committees and other occasions (Westlake 2006).

Another political check exercised upon the Commission is the subsidiarity check, or 'yellow-card' procedure established in the Constitutional Treaty and carried over to the Lisbon Treaty in a slightly different version. According to this yellow-card procedure, within six months of the issuing of a Commission legislative proposal (eight months in the Lisbon Treaty), when two-thirds of member states' national parliaments agree that the proposal violates the principle of subsidiarity, the Commission is forced to re-examine the proposal, though it is not obliged to withdraw it (that would be a 'red-card' procedure). Despite the Constitutional Treaty's uncertain future, on the initiative of NPs and with the organisational support of the Conference of Community and European Affairs Committees of Parliaments of the European Union (COSAC), the yellow-card procedure was established in practice in the months following the signing of the Treaty in the 2004 Inter-Governmental Conference (IGC). Pilot projects were commenced on the initiative of NPs with two directives related to cross-border divorce law and the liberalisation of postal services (COSAC web site).

While the Commission initially announced that it would not consider the procedure valid, it later issued a statement that it would take it into account. This shows the political force of the check. The Lisbon Treaty demonstrated the intention to further strengthen the check by NPs upon the Commission by introducing an 'orange-card' procedure. According to that procedure, if a majority of NPs objects to a Commission proposal, and the Commission still insists on pressing ahead with it, the EP and the Council can be called in to consider both sides of the argument and come up with a decision.

However, this is still not a red-card procedure – that is, the EP–Council decision could still overrule NPs.

Although the Commission is meant to be 'independent' from member states, it is checked by the Council both *ex ante* and in its everyday operation. Its *ex ante* check takes place in response to the Commission's proposals in the context of the legislative procedure. The everyday check takes place through comitology (see below).

In certain areas where the EP does not co-legislate, the Commission plays a significant management role, which is both administrative and political – for example, in the case of Lisbon Strategy management. The Council is at a disadvantage in checking the Commission, while the EP does not have the right to call the Commission to account, but only to provide opinions. The Commission thus has great leeway to act without effective checks. In its clearly administrative tasks, the Commission is checked internally, by the European Anti-Fraud Office (OLAF) and the European Ombudsman, and is supposed to be closely monitored by the EP.

Checks to the Council from NPs to their respective governments

In theory, the Council's individual members, though not the Council as a body (Lord and Harris 2006: 76), being national ministers are checked by the NPs that monitor the work of their respective governments. After the signing of the Single European Act in 1986, NPs became active in requesting information, setting up special EU committees and establishing scrutiny procedures to check their governments' role in EU affairs. At that time, the scope and range of EU regulation grew radically, and qualified majority voting (QMV) in the Council of Ministers – which meant that control of government decisions was rendered more difficult – became widespread (Norton 1996). Since the turn of the century, in view of the Constitutional debate, an important boost was given to the public perception of the role that NPs should play in checking their executives when acting in Council (Auel 2005). This is when enhanced information rights and the yellow-card procedure were established, attributing a more important role to NPs.

However, the major obstacle to the check that NPs can exercise upon their governments' actions in Council seems to be the continuing diversity of the scrutiny procedures of NPs, both as to their strength and as to their type (Harlow 2002: 85). Comparative studies, which have so far focused mainly on the EU-15, have emphasised the great diversity in relationships between parliaments and executives and the relative strength of parliaments with respect to their executives (Raunio 2005). Parliamentary traditions, general orientation of parliamentary political parties towards the EU (Maurer and Wessels 2001) and other factors account for why in some parliaments the check on their governments' decisions in the Council of Ministers is much weaker than in others.

Maurer and Wessels' comprehensive study of 2001, which examined each of the fifteen NPs, categorised them in four groups. The Danish, Swedish, Finnish and Austrian parliaments, in an effective and timely manner, formulate opinions and proposals about the daily business of the Union, are in a position to formulate and mandate a stance for the government in EU policy-making, and give out voting instructions. The Danish Folketing is the stronger of the four in the binding nature of its mandate to the government. A second group includes Germany and the Netherlands, which are also effective in following and preparing for EU policy-making, but given their consensual policy-making tradition and the EU consensus of the main political parties, this group does not allow parliamentarians to come into conflict with their governments over EU policy. A third group, consisting of the United Kingdom and French parliaments, is more modest in terms of the policy-making role it can play. This group does receive incoming information and can comment on draft positions of their respective governments through reports, resolutions or scrutiny reserves, but it cannot change the position that a government has decided to employ in Council. The fourth group, consisting of the NPs of Ireland, Belgium, Luxembourg, Greece, Portugal, Italy and Spain, is weak as to its capacity to process information and formulate positions on EU policy and is unwilling to challenge its governments on the positions that they take in Council. Rather it is deliberately supportive of its governments as long as interested parliamentarians can track EU policy-making and the role of their government in it. Differences can be discerned in timing as well. Some parliaments, notably those of the first group, are anticipatory and aim at formulating positions during the early stages of EU decision-making. Most others focus on scrutinising decisions *ex post*.

The status and role of established European affairs committees also differ. In some countries (Denmark, Finland, Austria, United Kingdom, Ireland) scrutiny on EU matters, specialised as they may be, is dealt with by the EU Affairs Committee exclusively and in full. In other countries (Sweden, Italy, Denmark, Netherlands), the EU Affairs Committee sifts through EU documentation to present the important issues to the specialised standing committees, while it mainly concerns itself with major EU issues such as enlargement and institutional reform (Maurer and Wessels 2001: 19–21).

The picture is one of continued heterogeneity, which is further enhanced with the entry of twelve new member states in 2004 and 2007. The exchange of best practices of scrutiny among NPs towards the governments in Council has intensified but is only of limited value, given the deep differences in parliamentary norms and culture, and has therefore done little so far to strengthen weaker parliaments in scrutinising their governments on its EU positions. This asymmetry of check would not be a problem if differences existed only in the specific form that practices take; the main problem lies with differences in strength, particularly between the first three groups of parliaments and the fourth group. When the Council decides by qualified majority, no decision can be taken without the agreement of governments that are not effectively checked (either *ex ante* or *ex post*) by their respective NPs.

The presidency of the Council is accountable to the EP, as it presents the presidency's programme at the beginning of its term and an account of what took place at the end of its term, while representatives of the presidency attend EP plenary sessions and answer MEPs' questions during its term of office. Between plenary sessions MEPs may address written questions to the Council, while ministers may attend EP committee meetings (Heyes-Renshaw 2006: 77).

Checks on the EU High Representative

Further complications are revealed on examination of a proposal, which was brought in with the Constitutional Treaty, regarding the establishment of the post of EU Foreign Minister (FM). According to the Treaty, this post would replace the CFSP High Representative's post, the holder of which is at present appointed by the member states and whose responsibilities are clearly demarcated to be within the second, intergovernmental pillar of the EU. The FM's responsibilities would be broader, as the purpose of the post would be to co-ordinate all aspects of the EU's external activities, economic and political. The FM would be appointed (and if necessary sacked) by the European Council by qualified majority. He or she would take part in the European Council and preside over the Council of General Affairs, while also taking up a vice-presidency in the European Commission. The Council would mandate the FM to carry out the Union's CFSP and Common Security and Defence Policy (CSDP), to the development of which they would be expected to contribute with proposals. As to the external activities that fall within the responsibility of the Commission the FM would be bound by Commission procedures. The Lisbon Treaty retains the substance of the post but reneges on the title of Foreign Minister, retreating to 'High Representative of the Union for Foreign Affairs and Security Policy', and delimits the incumbent's remit of responsibility to the pursuit and implementation of policies that have been unanimously agreed by the member states.

This leaves open several questions. To whom is the EU High Representative to be accountable? Will their appointment respect the principle, which holds for the president of the Commission, that they ought to come from the majority political block in the Parliament? Will they be considered a member of the College, at least with respect to its Commission-based responsibilities, which would mean that they would need to undergo the EP hearings procedure and *ex post* checks by the EP? Will they be a peer to other Commissioners and accountable to the Commission's president for its Commission-based responsibilities? On the other hand, if they are nominated and invested by, and therefore accountable to, the European Council for the CFSP and CSDP, will they also be accountable to the president for the Commission-based responsibilities? Even if this is indeed the case, to whom will they be responsible for the *co-ordination* of both sets of responsibilities? It is not unlikely that the check on the High Representative will be insufficient with respect to the overall co-ordination of EU external relations and activities or that there will be a tug-of-war between Commission and Council on who is supposed to check the High Representative on what.

Checks on the European Central Bank

The Governing Board of the European Central Bank (ECB) is a body that makes crucial decisions with key policy and political implications. The ECB's mandate – entrenched in the Treaty – is to enact anti-inflationary policy, arguably by prioritising price stability with respect to other economic policy goals, such as growth and employment. Its decisions with respect to interest rates affect millions of households across the EU and delimit national governments' economic policy decisions.

The ECB's leadership is completely independent. Its president is chosen by the governments of the member states and appointed by the EP. However, the ECB's president does not answer to the EP during their long term of office, and the minutes and votes are not published. Informally, presidents have been open to co-operation with the EP (McNamara 2006: 185–6). The president must present an annual report of the Bank's activity to the EP, Council and Commission and may request to be heard by the EP, as provided for in the Constitutional Treaty. Yet the presentation of that report receives no publicity or attention by the EU public at large. While it is certainly true that central banks are independent in most Western European economies, the ECB's independence is without precedent: in the EU there is no political counterpart that could provide a balancing check upon the Bank's priorities. The EP is weak from this point of view as there is as yet no clear political contestation of economic policy issues at European level to provide a political context for the ECB. The Eurogroup may be well positioned to play this role, but it does not include all the member states. Accountability is argued to be unnecessary by those who look upon legitimacy as strictly output legitimacy but necessary by those who consider that popular legitimacy through communication with the public is crucial and that national central bankers could fulfil such a role by communicating policy to the national publics. The EP itself has limited capacity to monitor the ECB, while the ECB's Executive Board deals with the question as if it were a one-way street, where policies need to be communicated downwards, rather than values and economic policy goals having to be communicated upwards.

Forum in the institutions of EU governance

Standards of political conduct differ across the EU, and common standards have not developed sufficiently. From the point of view of forum as set out above, this is a major problem. The shared practices of public contestation and deliberation in the context of which common standards might develop are rendered difficult in the first case because of the consensual style of EU politics and in the second case because of linguistic diversity and diversity of political culture. The development of EU-level media is thus hindered, and the potential recognisability of political representatives and therefore their distinctive public presence is limited. The background conditions for public justification of the allocation of rewards and punishments on the grounds of common political standards are therefore not present; nor is the allocation itself.

At this point it may be considered that this is not a real problem: the variety of national *fora* can be thought to effectively substitute for an EU-level forum. Alas, objections to this view that draw on the asymmetry of the allocation of rewards and punishments between the national and the European level can be raised. On the one hand, the allocation of rewards and punishments – that is, the public praise and blame, and the selection, appointment or non-reappointment of political representatives – by and large takes place at the national level, where EU issues are seen from the national perspective, mainly through the mechanisms of national political parties. On the other hand, for those issues which are clearly of European remit (such as the Union's economic, political and military role in the world), the European-level perspective on the discussion and allocation of rewards and punishments is underdeveloped. In other words, the allocation of rewards and punishments principally takes place at national level, though for several issues it should take place more clearly at EU level.

The EP as forum

The EP, which would be the natural forum for the Union, is not effective in debating, justifying and allocating sanction on grounds of desirable common political standards. If forum serves to assess and sanction the conduct of actors rather than acts, actors are not sufficiently recognisable in the context of the EP. Debate and justification before the public are problematic. Rewards and punishments are not for the EP to allocate.

Debate in the EP does take place, although it is indeed a debate characterised by diversity; the multitude of official languages, all of which are actually used in the plenary and the standing committees, is not conducive to initiating lively, direct and inspiring discussion that would allow common standards of political conduct to emerge. Apart from the diversity factor (but related to it), in most cases the politicians elected to the EP have been either young politicians in 'training' for the national arena or senior national political figures for whom EP membership represents honorary retirement. Until recently, few MEPs thought of the EP as a locus for a parliamentary career rather than as a passage to another political arena. Things are changing on this front; it has become evident during the last three European elections that about 30 per cent of MEPs aim at a European political career (Hix

2005: 90). The EP now has its own senior figures, who are highly influential in the standing committees and the plenary session. This became evident in the European Convention. Senior MEPs like Elmar Brok of the European Peoples' Party (EPP), the Liberal Andrew Duff, or Olivier Duhamel of the Party of European Socialists (PES) were among the 'movers and shakers' in the Convention plenary sessions (Norman 2003: 52–5).

Furthermore, the consensual style of politics in the EP has not offered great all-encompassing political contests at the plenary sessions. Again things may be changing here too. Recent empirical research shows that the increase in the legislative powers of the EP is intensifying political confrontation among 'Euro-parties' along the Left–Right axis (Hix *et al.* 2003). Furthermore, politicisation around the other major cleavage that characterises the EP party system – pro- and anti-integration – seems to be on the rise at the level of voter orientations, and its contestatory expression in both the European and national political arenas will largely depend on what political entrepreneurs make of it (van der Eijk and Franklin 2004: 48).

More serious, perhaps, is the lack of public attention that the EP's proceedings receive. In the past this was attributed to the fact that the EP often had to voice its concerns as a supranational institution aiming at greater institutional power rather than as a parliament that divides along partisan lines, as well as to the fact that elections to the EP are of second order (Hix 2005: 192–6). As some of these factors wane, or may be expected to wane, it becomes clearer that what is most at stake is the distance between European institutions and European citizens and the lack of a public sphere. Furthermore, the effectiveness of the debate in the EP is limited, insofar as there are no widespread European media and press to organise public debate at the European level.

Furthermore, the EP does not have major public rewards and punishments to give out. It allocates committee chairmanships and rapporteurships, and though these may be positions through which substantive policy influence can be exercised, they are not publicly acknowledged and the persons appointed are anyway filtered through the EP's party groups, which are in turn influenced by national parties (Mamadouh and Raunio 2003). Moreover, the EP cannot choose which politician, group or party gets given the post (or posts) of greater responsibility, as it does not have a decisive say as to the composition of the executive (Council and Commission). It cannot, as was mentioned, dismiss the College or individual Commissioners. It is, in fact, the Council that allocates rewards and punishments: it alone nominates the president of the Commission (though this may change), it appoints the members of the European Court of Justice, and its members separately nominate Commissioners and appoint members of the Committee of Permanent Representatives (COREPER), senior civil servants and comitology members. Furthermore, it is national rather than European parties that call the shots when it comes down to choosing those who are to run as MEPs for the EP. In general, it is predominantly at the national, and not at the European, level that debate and public justification take place and that punishments and rewards are allocated.

The Convention method

First the European Charter of Human Rights and then, more prominently, the Constitutional Treaty were openly debated in *ad hoc* fora, which included representatives from all of the Union's institutions, national governments and parliaments, stakeholders and civil society associations. It can be argued that the Convention method represents a comprehensive, inclusive forum where important questions for the Union and the future of European integration can to some extent become the object of open public deliberation (Magnette 2004). As in the case of open co-ordination, the Convention method may be thought of as a public process whereby common standards of political conduct are built up through contestation and deliberative interaction.

Yet one may ask what kinds of punishment and reward can be given out by the Convention method. As the Convention progressed, the president's conduct was described as 'authoritarian', the Commission's contribution was characterised as 'insufficient', and some member state representatives, national parliamentarians or MEPs were said to have stood out for playing a 'uniting', 'inspiring' or 'disruptive' role. Given that the Convention is not a regularly enacted but an *ad hoc* event, the types of reward and punishment allocated involve merely public rebuke or praise. There are no direct repercussions concerning the allocation of public office.

EU policy-making fora

Joerges and Neyer have argued that comitology – that is, the system of committee governance that supports the work of the Commission, the Council and the EP – represents an emerging 'deliberative supranationalism' where national and European officials consensually and efficiently manage EU policy-making. They depict comitology as a forum where deliberation, rather than inter-governmental bargaining, is the norm (Joerges and Neyer 1997; Joerges 2002). Likewise, organised dialogue with civil society at EU level has been portrayed as a forum for debate, consultation and deliberation with respect to policy-making (Commission 2001). Finally, the open method of co-ordination has been argued to constitute a case of democratic experimentalist forum, in the context of which member states debate, exchange best practices and engage in mutual learning with the assistance of the European Commission (Sabel and Zeitlin 2007). Benchmarking, peer review and open 'naming and shaming' are designed to entice member states into better performance and gradual, voluntary, policy convergence (Borrás and Jacobsson 2004).

For the purposes of accountability as set out above, forum is about assessing agents against common standards of political conduct and allocating punishments and rewards before the public eye. Neither deliberation in comitology nor consultation with organised civil society qualify as forum in this sense. Deliberations held in the context of these practices are not public, either in the sense that proceedings are not necessarily held in public or in the sense that they cannot be followed by the general public because they are too technical or too specialised. Moreover there are no common standards of political conduct at stake or public allocation of rewards and punishments. Things are different with the open method of co-ordination. Subject to the general limitations of the European public sphere, as well as to the complex and technical nature of the process, open co-ordination works towards the construction of common standards of political conduct and offers rewards and punishments through public naming and shaming. It can therefore be argued to hold potential as a European-level forum.

National fora

Do NPs suffice as fora in the context of which public deliberation on the grounds of common standards of political conduct and the allocation of punishments and rewards can take place with respect to the EU as a whole? Can they in this sense be argued to cover for the EP's weakness to operate from this point of view? NPs do have public rewards and punishments to give out with respect to European issues not only involving praise and reproach but also concerning the promotion to a more important office or demotion from one. Nonetheless, they do this according to national standards of political conduct, to national politicians, over what are essentially perceived as national issues.

In practice, comparative studies have shown that NPs differ as to the extent to which they can debate European-level questions (Auel 2007) and as to which European-level questions they debate. A Bruegel Report concerning the extent to which NPs owned up to the reform of the Lisbon Strategy demonstrated that there are considerable differences (Pisani-Ferry and Sapir 2006). The Constitutional Treaty was debated in some NPs more than in others. Their operation as fora debating EU issues is therefore uneven and diverse.

Moreover, NPs are more likely to debate policy questions that are more relevant to their country's interest and hierarchy in the national agenda – for instance, the EU's foreign policy, agricultural policy or structural funds. Broader EU questions such as the Constitutional Treaty, enlargement, or the Union's role in the world are also more likely to be debated from the national perspective and perception of interests (Hüller 2007: 572–4). In other words, national assemblies may debate European problems but lack the European perspective.

Finally, there is the question of common standards of political conduct. Clearly, national difference is crucial here. Yet when compared with the open method of co-ordination or the Convention method, debates in NPs do not constitute the *loci* where common European standards of political conduct are coined. Rather they are the hubs of national standards of political conduct, which may receive some influence from other NPs or from EU institutions. The new information rights and the yellow- or orange-card procedure go some way towards offering a platform for intra-parliamentary forum of NPs on European-level questions, even if debate is supposed to be limited to subsidiarity questions.

National referenda on EU questions, such as membership or Treaty approval, can be argued to provide a more open, public and focused means of debate at national level with wider implications for the Union. National debates on national referenda over EU issues have the potential to affect equivalent national debates in other member states, as the French debate on the Constitutional Treaty arguably has. The problem still remains that, for the most part, the perspective is national and therefore the debate is second-order as well.

Conclusion

It has been argued in this chapter that a system of governance requires both check and forum as institutional features if the practice of political accountability is to be effective. This is contrary to most contemporary approaches, which overemphasise check and neglect forum. In the EU's institutional setup forum seems to be weaker than check, owing by and large to the asymmetry in the allocation of rewards and punishments between levels of governance. At national level, fora debate and provide the background to assigning rewards and punishments for European-level matters from a national perspective, while at the same time the European-level public sphere is weak and the EU's capacity to allocate rewards and punishments meagre. This is not to say that no questions remain over check in the EU's institutional setup. No clear overall model of checks has been established in what concerns the EU's core institutional structure, while new accountability gaps are argued to have emerged in the operation of the ECB and in the establishment of new posts such as that of the EU High Representative.

4

Identifiability

Introduction

Identifiability is a feature of the organisation of political institutions which ensures that the following question can always be answered in the operation of a system of governance: who was responsible? This is an important political question – especially when things go wrong. If it cannot be answered, accountability is rendered impossible (Beaud 2000: 24). It is therefore important to explore how we go about answering the identifiability question. Two accounts of how one is to answer will be put forward: the 'causal' and 'institutional' accounts. It will be argued that the causal account runs into trouble when confronted with the problem of 'many hands'. The institutional account is more helpful despite the fact that it runs up against the problem of 'personification'.

From the institutional account, we argue that if the mechanism of identifiability is to be effective, it requires, firstly, that the formal institutional structure of a system of governance be stable, simple and clear, and secondly, that two informal norms be adhered to: that agents keep to their roles and that they accept responsibility for their role requirements. The first requirement refers to the appropriate characteristics of the distribution of responsibility in a system of governance, whereas the second refers to the appropriateness of political agents' acceptance of this distribution. Identifiability fails when these requirements are not met. Finally, the EU will be examined as to whether it meets the requirements of identifiability.

The causal account of locating political responsibility

When an attempt is made to locate political responsibility, it is common to try to 'pin' it on someone, to examine which person or persons 'brought about' a certain political outcome. We use these terms to locate responsibility in political activity in the same way as we use them for legal or professional liability and in our general moral discourse. This can be referred to as the causal account of political responsibility. According to this account, to be responsible for a certain outcome is to be the distinctive and effective cause of that outcome through one's intentional action, or (under certain conditions) inaction, and given the absence of compulsion or ignorance (Aristotle, *NE*: III0a–III5a, 44).

Under this definition, the agent of responsibility, if they are reasonably to be considered as such, must possess certain capacities. If we suppose that these capacities must include the ability to receive and classify information, the faculty of reason and the minimal requirements of judgement, only persons – singly or acting together – can possess such capacities, and therefore only persons can bear responsibility. When we ask who is responsible for a certain outcome, we are looking for a cause, and this cause is the action or inaction of a person. Alternatively, we may be looking for a set of co-causes that clearly form a cause, and this cause is one or more actions (or inactions), with identifiable parts, by a group of persons in bringing about the outcome. If one person through their actions is the sole or the effective cause of a certain outcome, then that person's responsibility for that outcome is clear and it is to be borne completely by that person. If there are many persons acting together, then the part held by each person in the shared responsibility can (at least in principle) be traced back to each one in proportion to their contribution in bringing about the outcome (Feinberg 1970: 243–8).

All this, of course, supposes that there are outcomes that can be brought about by the intentional action of a person alone, or by a number of persons whose contribution is distinguishable. For example, if I, standing on a hill just above you, throw a stone with the intention that it should fall on your head and kill you, and you die, then I have the whole responsibility for your death. Or, if a group of us conspires to rob a bank, then we will each have our personal moral responsibility for our own part in the robbery and shared responsibility as a group.

The problem of 'many hands'

Particularly when it is applied to political outcomes, the causal account of responsibility is likely to run into trouble. Consider the following situation: Party A, consisting of individuals who chose to be members of the party, acting collectively, was defeated in the national elections. If we employed the causal account, we would have to find out which was the person (or persons) responsible for this political outcome. The questions we would ask – were we to follow this line of reasoning – would be: whose fault is it that the party was defeated? Who did something wrong, or didn't do enough? In other words, which person or persons are causally responsible for the party's defeat? And when more than one person is found to be responsible, we would expect to be able to apportion responsibility among them in a clear and fair way. The problems become apparent immediately.

Party A is something more than the sum of its present members. It has a history, a commitment to certain ideals and symbols, a certain continuity. It carries much of its past with it and it commits the persons that are currently its members to the mistakes as well as the achievements of their predecessors in the party. It has a certain political 'capital', an *inheritance*, which its members share, claim, reshape, exploit and are bound together by. Inheritance is important in setting decisive limits on what the current members of the party can do or propose to do. No single person (or group of persons) is causally responsible for this inheritance, but through their membership they can be said to accept some of the burden of justifying the mistakes of their predecessors, to the degree that they accept the credit for their achievements.

When it is necessary, party members decide on the shape that the political alternative put forward by the party will take. They do this through collective deliberation and debate, as well as through internal power struggles and the handling of internal balances of all kinds. The subject matter of these debates is not simply their own personal opinions or interests (or both): they draw on what they understand to be relevant in other people's opinions and interests outside the party. Each party member's contribution to this process of formation of political alternative is not easily discernible, to the point where it is doubtful whether it is discernible at all. This is because contributions vary not only in degree but also in kind. A small contribution may nevertheless be a significant one. Members are each partly 'co-causes' (Goldman 1999: 201–17) of what non-members perceive as the party's political alternative – that is, a more or less coherent account of what things are like for us all and what should be done about them. But non-members are also co-causes of this perceived alternative, since party members agreed to it and discussed it with their demands and views in mind.

It may be asked where leadership fits in, and whether a leader or the leading party group should not bear greater responsibility for the political alternative that comes out in the end. Although party members do choose their leadership, or consent to it, they never give up all their power to their leadership. Their continuous mobilisation and support is necessary for the very existence of the party, let alone its leadership. Party leadership does play a role in terms of personal characteristics and qualities, and this role, in varying degrees, can be said to be an important co-cause of the form that the political alternative will take. However, the claims that party leadership is what the power struggle or the deliberative process in the party is all about, or that it is the leadership that brings about the emergence of a certain alternative, are not beyond dispute; rather, it can be argued that the choice of leadership is an expression of the alternative that the members, or a majority of the members, embrace or accept, insofar as it articulates this alternative.

There are other factors that shape the political alternative that the party will present to the public – factors that may be of even greater importance to its formation than the leadership, or even the party members as a group: possible or actual alternatives that are better – or simply more *convincing* – may play a devastating role, already at the formation stage of a party's proposed political alternative. In any case, when political proposals are formed they take into account their rivals, potential or actual. These rivals, and through them their bearers, are also co-causes of the political alternative that results. Again, there is no easy way to tell in what way and to what intensity one external counter-alternative – formed by the same process by which party A's alternative was formed – contributed more than another to the formation of the party's political alternative. These alternatives enter inter-party deliberation and decision processes, leading to one direction rather than another. Deliberation on alternatives introduces a qualitative element that remains vague with regard to the persons involved as causes. Assuming that each person can be associated with a particular view, when the battle of discussion is over, it is hard to say who – as an individual – was more influential in their input and therefore who contributed more to the outcome. This is because people may change their mind and their stance during the process of deliberation; they may be convinced of another view. Also, the result may be one of synthesis and compromise rather than the domination of a winner.

Even if we could find which person or persons bore the causal responsibility or, at best, most of the causal responsibility for the resulting political alternative, we would still have to see how and to what extent we can attribute electoral defeat to the political alternative that was put forward and to what extent we can attribute that defeat to other causes, like one-off events that were external to the party, or changes in the party system, and so on. Moreover, we need to examine how the party handled its political alternative in the pre-election period; how effective its efforts were to convince, how it handled the competition, and so on. Again, it is difficult to attribute causal responsibility to individual persons since contributions in a campaign vary qualitatively to a considerable degree. One contributes financially, another by putting posters on walls, another by convincing people, yet another by coming up with bright ideas, and so on. It is not possible to measure the extents of these different contributions in a quantifiable and comparable way.

The picture that emerges is not one where causal responsibility can be pinned directly on particular persons – whether members or non-members of the party – for particular deeds or omissions, which led to the electoral defeat of Party A in clearly distinguishable ways and degrees. It seems that responsibility in causal terms for particular political outcomes is blurred to such an extent that it becomes something that cannot be said in any meaningful way to be held by specific persons for specific outcomes. Thompson has called this the 'problem of many hands' (Thompson 1980: 905–16). Speaking about government and public officials, he describes the problem as follows:

> Because many different officials contribute in many ways to decisions and policies of the government, it is difficult even in principle to identify who is morally responsible for political outcomes. (Thompson 1980: 905)

The problem of many hands is not unusual in contemporary politics, administration and the activities of large organisations. Complexity, size and the collective nature of these activities all contribute to the fact that the problem of many hands is quite common. Causal responsibility for political outcomes is tendentially collective, because political problems and political action are both collective (Beaud 2000: 26). In his discussion of complex organisations, public and private, Bovens has identified the problem of many hands as being the principal problem (in the causal account) of responsibility (Bovens 1998: 45–50). Given, then, the problem of many hands, how can we locate responsibility for political outcomes?

The causal account of responsibility will generate two answers, neither of which gives useful insights. One answer would be that no one was responsible; if only individuals can bear responsibility and if in order to establish collective responsibility we must refer back to the responsibility of individuals and demonstrate how (and how much) each individual was responsible for an outcome, then in a situation where we cannot distinguish individual responsibility, it follows that collective responsibility cannot be established either. It is obvious that this is not an attractive option from the point of view of identifiability. A second answer would be to say that everyone – individually and collectively – was responsible for the outcome. Given the problem of many hands, causal responsibility for political outcomes may not be traceable to specific persons for specific political outcomes, yet it involves all the persons that comprise a political community. Therefore, in accordance with the causal account of responsibility, we should consider everybody, including ourselves, responsible for particular political outcomes. Surely it is not equally and in full that each person bears this collective responsibility – individual contributions are asymmetrical – but it is, nevertheless, a responsibility borne by all individuals insofar as all individuals are to some extent involved in politics through their actions or omissions.

This second answer may be valuable in terms of political morality. Responsibility as a collective asset backs the projects of any given political community and allows it to 'collectivise' the risks of the common political enterprise. Rarely has any good, or even significant, political outcome been brought about without a generalised sense of responsibility. Generalised support for the welfare state, for the financing of environmental protection and cultural projects, the organised resistance to a dictatorship, many social movements, certain forms of organised voluntary activity, and participation in democratic elections in the absence of compulsory voting are but a few examples. To think of responsibility in those terms is to think of it in moral terms, and to endorse it is a moral enterprise that is important to every community. But valuable as a generalised sense of individual and collective responsibility may be, it is no more use as a solution to the identifiability problem than the first alternative. If these are the answers that the causal account of responsibility provides to the identifiability question arising from the problem of many hands, then the causal account is inadequate.

The institutional account of locating political responsibility

H. S. Richardson supports the notion of institutionally divided responsibility as opposed to the notion of responsibility which remains unvaried across persons or roles (Richardson 1999: 218–49).

> The moral agent's responsibility depends upon regular features of her social situation and role, as shaped by the moral rules themselves, and carries with it delimited authorisations, varying systematically with her situation and role, to depart from our (pre-existing best assessment of the) moral rules. (Richardson 1999: 225)

The way to locate responsibility, according to this passage, involves looking in two directions. First, we must look towards the institutional structure and see what requirements a role makes upon a particular agent:

> It depends on the structure, the environment, and the culture of an organisation, along which lines responsibility inside the organisation is regulated. (Bovens 1998: 51)

Then, we must look towards the agent and see whether they departed from their role requirements, and if so, whether this departure was authorised, to what extent and in what way:

> the imputation of responsibility will differ from person to person, whether one is at the top or at the bottom of the organisational hierarchy, one is judged on the basis of one's personal conduct. (Bovens 1998: 106)

So far, so good. We know how to approach the identifiability question and where to look when we are trying to locate responsibility. But the institutional approach presupposes two things: that there is a structure of roles that we can reliably point to in the first place and that agents acknowledge, accept and adhere to this structure of roles. In other words, identifiability according to the institutional approach requires formal institutions to be set up in such a way that it is possible to distinguish who is supposed to do what and when, and the presence of norms that bind agents to uphold this system of roles. These are the requirements of identifiability – that is, the organisational principle that enables us to answer the question: who was responsible? Each of these requirements will be examined in turn.

The distribution of responsibility among roles

Political responsibility takes the 'shape' of the particular system of interactions that occur among political roles. In other words, political responsibility is distributed among political roles in accordance with the way in which the system of interactions among roles operates. This shape can be typically seen in the formal institutional structure of a polity, although it is not restricted to its formal characteristics. Informal interactions, norms, ways of doing things and standard operating procedures within political organisations may all be included in the description of how the system of political roles is organised.

The distribution of political responsibility among political roles in a system of governance cannot be compared to the collective responsibility for political outcomes among persons belonging to a political community, since the former operates at a different, more mediated, level of interaction. From this point of view, the danger of irresponsibility in politics comes not from the diffusion of responsibility among persons but from the fluidity or solidity of the shape that political responsibility takes among political roles. In other words, what we commonly perceive as the danger of political irresponsibility is due to lack of clarity and simplicity in the design of political systems as systems of political roles (Price, 1985: 136), or to lack of stability in the system of political roles, not to the diffusion of responsibility among persons. Clarity, simplicity and stability are therefore required in a system of roles if we are to be able to answer the identifiability question at the institutional level.

Clarity in the system of roles implies that it must be made generally known who is supposed to perform a particular role; what requirements the role makes upon its occupant; in what circumstances the role occupant is supposed to carry out the role's requirements; and to what extent and in what way the role occupant can depart from those requirements. The limits of the role must be known – that is, where it begins and ends, or when a task must be performed by this particular role occupant and not by another. In other words, the system of roles must be such that the role occupant knows what they are supposed to do and that others can know what that person is expected to do.

As for simplicity, in a complex organisation a system of roles must be as simple as possible, which means that it must comprise as few roles, or categories of roles, as possible. Joint tasks involving more than one role must avoid overlapping and duplication; and the terms of co-operation among roles must be limited to as few cases and procedures as possible. Co-ordination and sanction must be performed by as few centres as possible. Precision in the briefing of tasks aids simplicity; so does parsimony.

Turning to stability, it should be said that stability does not mean the same as immobility:

> institutions, or structures, are patterns of behaviour that persist over time, but they are never exactly the same after the passage of time. What makes them recognisable as institutions is the fact that they show a basic stability and continuity, which allows them to adapt to changing circumstances without losing their identity. (Vile 1967: 344)

Systems of roles change, and have to change, because old tasks become redundant and new ones must be dealt with. Instability may well be justified, for example, when radical change leads to the rearrangement of the system of political roles (Gregory 1998: 519–38). Under normal conditions, stability means that role occupants know what they are supposed to be doing in the foreseeable future and that role requirements do not change from one day to another. It also means that when role requirements do change their occupants are adequately prepared to deal with the change.

In order, then, for identifiability to be possible on the institutional side, the distribution of responsibility among roles must be clearly defined, as simple as possible and relatively stable.

Norms of adherence to a role and acceptance of responsibility for role-related duties

The requirement that a clear, simple and stable distribution of political responsibility be 'written into' the structure of roles is not enough for the functioning of the mechanism of identifiability – that is, as a guaranteed way of answering the identifiability question. Even if an ideal distribution of political responsibility is in place for all to see, agents still must generally adhere to it; for what good would such a distribution do if, when it came down to it, role occupants did not abide by it? What would happen if role occupants continuously fought amongst themselves for tasks, if they constantly meddled in others' tasks, or if they did not carry out some of their tasks systematically? Finally, what would ensue if they did not accept responsibility for those tasks, if they always blamed someone else for what was their business to have taken care of, or if they systematically exploited the problem of many hands in order to shift responsibility to others?

Although such a generalised state of affairs is not easy to imagine, it is possible to point to cases of such behaviour in many systems. We often hear of ministers who refuse to take responsibility for policy blunders, accidents or fiascos that take place within 'their' policy area. This was by and large also the case with several Commissioners in the episode of the Santer Commission's resignation. When such phenomena are the exception rather than the rule and when they are frowned upon rather than applauded, this indicates the presence of certain norms that dictate that each role occupant should stick to doing their own part and take responsibility for that part. When such cases are systematically treated with indifference or with tolerance, then these norms are either not operative or not binding enough.

The problem of personification

If the presence of these norms is necessary to the institutional approach, then we may have run into some trouble. This is because the problem of many hands, which discredits the causal responsibility approach, gives rise to another problem which undermines the norms of adhering to one's role-related tasks and taking responsibility for them. This problem, which here will be dubbed the problem of personification, is the following: when we try to locate political responsibility, we find it difficult to comprehend the abstract entity of a role occupant. We need to think that we are looking for a person. We need to *personify* political responsibility, to act *as if* a person or a group of persons were really causally responsible for a particular political outcome. We personify political responsibility in order to evaluate political agency and understand political issues (Magnette 2006: 35) and to work out the ways in which the two are related. This need arises because we think in terms of reasons, and reasons are always produced by a person or of a group of people. Furthermore, we think in terms of motivation, and motivation is always personal; the assignment of sanction through praise and blame is typically designed to address, and is received at the level of, personal motivation. Finally, we need to see a person in order to be able to recognise, in them and by their actions, conduct that we can comprehend and assess; we cannot do that in the absence of a face, a character.

On the other hand, a person who occupies a role knows well that the causal responsibility account is wrong: they know that the causes of political outcomes are complex and that their own contribution to them is in any case limited, whatever the scope for freedom that their role allows. A minister may decide on the direction of policy, but their period of office is normally short. Ministers are well aware that they have to act on an inherited situation, that their success often depends on the success of other ministers, that they can only chose a small proportion of their staff, and that the staff could well be saying, 'Yes, Minister', only to carry out business in their own way after the minister's back is turned. Ministers cannot reasonably oversee every detail of the implementation of their proposals, although they are expected to in principle. However, it is part of their role-related duties to take responsibility for a bad outcome, as much as it is part of their role-related rewards to take credit for a good outcome.

Normally, when we try to locate responsibility, we first look at who did not do (or did badly) what they were supposed to do. It is the person in that role whom we seek to hold responsible, not someone whose role had nothing to do – institutionally – with the outcome in question. Normally, then, the person involved will have had *some* causal responsibility for the outcome. But, as was argued earlier in this chapter, that person will normally not have held *all* the causal responsibility. Systems of governance whose purpose is to regulate differentiated mass societies are characterised by high levels of impersonality and complexity. This generates problems for the personification of responsibility: on the one hand, we need to know that persons are found responsible and that persons accept this responsibility; on the other hand, it is difficult for persons to accept the responsibility since they know that it is not all theirs to take. This is the problem of personification.

At this point, if identifiability is to become possible, a theatre or a ritual of personification of political responsibility is rendered necessary (Gregory 1998: 531–3): we must pretend that particular persons are the causes of political outcomes, even if (as was explained in the first section) in politics, their responsibility cannot be individuated in causal terms. Furthermore

– and this is what interests us here – role occupants must undertake themselves to pretend that they are indeed the causes of political outcomes, as ministers sometimes do when they resign on account of the slip-ups of their subordinates. However, this raises several questions: what is the normative standing of this virtual reality? Why should we continue to consider particular persons causally responsible for particular political outcomes even if we know they are not? And why should role occupants agree to undertake such a disproportionate burden of responsibility, even though they know better than anybody the real extent of their share? According to Kertzer,

> [We] live in a world that must be drastically simplified if it is to be understood at all; political rituals give us a way to understand it. (Kertzer 1988: 2)

Through the ritual of personifying responsibility it becomes possible to express and vindicate the standards of the political community in public; in other words, it becomes possible to expose to public assessment our own common standards of political conduct and to debate the question of what kind of people we want to be as political beings and what kind of political beings our institutions should be designed to foster. Furthermore, in impersonal systems, when something goes wrong, trust in the system as a whole may be damaged, and the ritual provides a valuable way of ensuring that the damage is attributed to a particular source (Jimenez 1998: 85). Finally, blaming those in positions of responsibility may serve in a pre-emptive capacity: it may make them more inclined to do more to avoid problems in the future (Schklar 1990: 64-5). These are the reasons that justify our part in the game, which consists of seeking a responsible party, and it is against the background of these reasons that identifiability can be distinguished from the Christian notion of looking for sinners (Smiley 1992: 63), as well as from the blind communal practice of scapegoating (Schklar 1990: 4).

What of political agents undertaking full responsibility even if it is not theirs to take? Firstly, as Fischer and Ravizza argue in their discussion of moral responsibility, 'when a person takes responsibility, he is "asking" the moral community to recognise him as a legitimate participant in ... moral conversation' (Fischer and Ravizza 1998: 214). The case is analogous in 'political' conversation: accepting responsibility means asking for public acknowledgement that one is a legitimate participant in the political game. Secondly, political agents must take the rough with the smooth; their role positions imply risks as well as rewards. Among them is the risk of being found responsible for something they did not do, or did not do alone. Through the privileges of their office they stand the chance of being rewarded, but they also risk being punished and it would not be appropriate for them to take only the privileges attached to their role but not the dangers. We might think that undertaking to personify political responsibility is part of the political agent's role-related duties, whether this is made explicit or not.

The problem of personification is, then, a threat to the norms of adherence to tasks and acceptance of responsibility for those tasks. Agents can reasonably claim that their tasks were impossible to fulfil in the first place and that they should not be held responsible for them. Sometimes they are right. But they cannot pick and choose; they must take the bad with the good. The problem of personification is resolved with the construction of a false reality, where those who seek to locate responsibility act *as if* particular persons are causally responsible for political outcomes, and those who accept causal responsibility act *as if* it was indeed their responsibility. This false reality is justifiable in normative terms.

If, then, personification is not a problem for the institutional account, it can be concluded that the institutional account indeed provides a good instrument for locating responsibility. According to the institutional account, identifiability requires that the distribution of political responsibility among roles be clear, simple and stable, and that norms be in place that dictate agents' acceptance of their tasks and assumption of responsibility for them. It is now possible to examine whether these requirements are met in the EU system of governance.

Identifiability in the EU

Arguably, lack of identifiability is the most pronounced failure of responsibility in the EU, and the instances in which it can be observed are numerous, both in the institutional configuration of political roles and in the norms supportive of identifiability. The Union's continuous evolution through Treaty reforms in the process of European Integration, and also (and mainly) through the piecemeal steps inherited by the Monnet method, have been detrimental to the clarity, simplicity and stability of political roles. Constitutionalisation of the EU as such acquires great importance from this point of view, as does the modality of constitutional reform as conceived in the Constitutional Treaty.

The interrelations between the main institutions are burdened horizontally by the complexity of a checks and balances system and vertically by the lack of a clear allocation of competences to each level of governance (Micklitz and Weatherhill 1994: 31). One specific area that was singled out for attention in, and as a result of, the Constitutional debate concerns the debate over the merits of having a competence catalogue from the point of view of simplicity and clarity. Another area concerns the unclear and unduly complex distribution of roles in the executive among the president of the European Commission, the new European Council president and the presidencies of the various Council formations, and the Foreign Minister.

The multitude, diversity and multi-level character of decision-making modes, the technical nature of much of the Union's work and the non-hierarchical network-like texture of governance are further obstacles to simplicity and clarity. The attempt to simplify legislative procedures and types of acts, as well as the major unresolved issue of comitology, are crucial here. The trend to avoid further complexity has been reflected in the rejection of the creation of new parliamentary chambers in the EU and new collective bodies more generally.

On the other hand, the development of norms concerning the need to keep to a designated role and to accept responsibility falls way behind developments on the institutional side. Even if the institutional structure were attuned to identifiability, institutional agents at the EU level would need to develop the sort of constitutional culture of self-restraint with regard to claiming power that is characteristic of federal systems. Assumption of responsibility would require elected politicians of European remit and national governments that would refrain from playing 'two-level games' with their EU partners when trying to pass unpopular reforms.

Constitutionalisation versus the Monnet method

Establishing a constitution for the European Union went against the grain of what fifty years of step-by-step integration by means of the Monnet method had stood for. What distinguishes constitution-making from functional integration is the firmness and explicitness of the political statement involved. For European federalists, longstanding advocates of constitution-making, the terms of the commitment that the European states and peoples would be bound by had to be open, stable, clear, precise, and consolidated through political debate and explicit political approval if the constitution were to command legitimacy and be understood (Burgess 1986). Changes to the constitution had also to take place in the same manner that the constitution was to be established, irrespective of how easy it would be to bring about change: by straightforward political agreement. By contrast, the functionalist strategy involved bypassing the political process altogether, fragmenting sovereignty and handing various pieces of it to supranational centres of power at appropriate moments. Change was not meant to take place by political agreement, but gradually and piece by piece, according to emerging opportunity rather than according to fixed rules or principles, driven by anonymous technocratic elites.

Decades of integration 'by stealth' (Hayward 1996) or competence 'creep' (Pollack 1995) have brought about confusion about the level of governance and the institutions responsible for decision-making in different policy areas. The formal and informal rules according to which each of the major institutions of the Union exercises its political role, and therefore the confines of political roles themselves, are largely unstable. Moreover, it is also the tasks attached to political roles that change continuously: political agents are always called upon to take on new tasks in the process of integration – for example, the Commission in the Delors period, the EP through the expansion of co-decision, and the Council with new governance methods such as the Open Method of Co-ordination (OMC). They may also be asked to perform their tasks in a different way – for instance, changes in decision rules and procedures such as the shift from unanimity to QMV in the Council. It is therefore difficult to speak of political roles as having stable contents that both political agents themselves and their political audience can sensibly follow.

After the Treaty of Maastricht, the principle of subsidiarity was established as a means to address 'competence creep'. According to the principle: 'the Community shall take action … only if and insofar as the objectives of the proposed action cannot be sufficiently achieved by the member states and can therefore, by reason of the scale or effects of the proposed action, be better achieved by the Community' (*Treaty establishing the European Community* 1997: Article 3b). Subsidiarity succeeded in making competence creep more difficult to some extent, but it soon became obvious that it would not be enough to provide adequate answers to the question of clarity and simplicity. It turned out to be a principle about how to use existing competences and not a mechanism for clarifying 'who does what' in the Union.

The Constitutional Convention signalled the emergence of the constitutional route as a serious alternative to piecemeal integration. One of the major reasons for which a considerable part of the EU's political elites called for a constitution was exactly the perceived need to set out a 'power map' (Duchacek 1973: 3–5) that would strengthen identifiability in the Union's institutional structure. Constitutions assign powers, and by so doing they give shape and structure to governance and they set out how these powers can be employed. From this point of view, constitutions provide for a clear, simple and stable plan of what political agents are meant to do, on their own and in relation to each other, which allows citizens to locate political responsibility. Unfortunately for identifiability in the EU, this aspect of the Constitutional Treaty has not survived the failure to validate the Treaty through referenda.

The Constitutional Treaty also addressed the question of constitutional change, and therefore the stability of political roles, by introducing two mechanisms intended to control competence creep and a new method for constitutional reform. The mechanisms were the early warning system set out in the subsidiarity protocol and the 'passerelle' clause. The principles of conferral, subsidiarity and proportionality are stated in the Constitutional Treaty as the principles according to which competences are to be exercised. Two subsidiarity protocols establishing the increased information rights for national parliaments, upgraded to 'watchdogs' of subsidiarity and the 'early warning system', are annexed to the Constitutional Treaty. The flexibility, or 'passerelle', clause of Art. I-18 enables the Union to act beyond its scope of competence in unforeseen circumstances, only after two conditions have been met: first, that unanimity has been mustered in the Council, and second, that member states' national parliaments have been informed explicitly in advance. Finally, the Convention method, involving public debate and deliberation involving all major players in the European Union (the Institutions, member state governments and parliaments), became a precedent for subsequent major constitutional reforms.

Can these innovations be expected to suffice in protecting against competence creep, thus safeguarding the relative stability of political roles? In order to answer the question we must think of constitution-making in the European Union (and beyond) not as a one-off agreement but as an ongoing and contested process (Wiener and de la Sala 1997; Shaw 2003). A promising trend can be discerned towards such an understanding of constitutional change as a political, as opposed to legal or technical process. All three mechanisms of constitutional change are by and large political mechanisms that – at least in principle - require public debate and explicit political agreement before major changes can be made. In this sense, they are more in line with what federalists as opposed to functionalists would applaud.

Cataloguing competences

The European Union has been based on a system of enumerated competences. It has those competences conferred upon it by the Treaties and primary law. Before the Constitutional Treaty, those competences could be classified as exclusive and non-exclusive, only the latter being subject to the principle of subsidiarity. There were no formal lists of competences as in federal constitutions; rather, competence provisions were scattered all over the Treaties (Mayer 2004).

Fischer's 2000 Berlin speech on federalism in the EU (Fischer 2000) and pressures by the German Länder (Mayer 2004) renewed discussions on articulating a formal catalogue of competences in the European Union, along the lines of federal constitutions. The discussion touched on several key issues about the future of the European Union, not least its *finalité politique*: was Europe to become federal, confederal or a federation of member states (Crum 2003)? The Laeken Declaration, which set out the main tasks that the European Convention was meant to address, reflecting concern with the division of labour between levels of governance, stated that one of the Convention's aims should be to enhance the Union's understandability to citizens (and therefore their capacity to locate political responsibility) by simplifying the competence system (Laeken Declaration 2001).

The Constitutional Treaty did not introduce a detailed competence catalogue that would state competence in detail for each policy area. Rather, it went for a system of delineated categories of powers (de Búrca and de Witte 2002: 207–13). A specific title was introduced in Part I of the Constitutional Treaty, which states and describes the different categories of Union competences, distinguishing between 'exclusive', 'shared' and 'supporting, co-ordinating or complementary' competences, while competence provisions from the previous Treaties are maintained without major substantive changes in Part III, where policies are described in detail.

'Exclusive' competences, in which only the Union can act, include: competition rules for the internal market; monetary policy; common commercial policy; the customs union; and the conservation of marine bio-logical resources under the common fisheries policy. Under 'shared' competences in which both the Union and member states can act, the policy areas listed are: the internal market; the area of freedom, security and justice; agriculture and fisheries; transport; trans-European networks; energy; certain aspects of social policy; economic and social cohesion; environment; and common safety concerns in public health matters. 'Supporting, co-ordinating and complementary' measures, where the Union can for the most part make only non-binding recommendations, include industry; protection and improvement of human health; education; vocational training; youth and sport; culture; and civil protection. Apart from this threefold general classification of competences, separate articles are dedicated to the co-ordination of economic and social policies of the member states, the CFSP and external competences of the Union, which are understood to reflect the particular characteristics of Union competence in these areas.

Is the Union's categorisation of powers likely to enhance identifiability in the European Union? In terms of clarity and simplicity, the catalogue does indeed improve the situation. Mayer argues, though, that the policy areas listed are too general and that it is necessary to turn to Part III to understand which aspect of which policies fall under which category of competences. He also says that it is rather confusing to interpolate articles on the co-ordination of social and economic policies and the CFSP between the more general categories of competence. Furthermore, that competences were not more clearly defined and allocated between member states and the European Union is due to the fact that on the one hand no major substantive changes were made in terms of (re-)nationalisation of competences while on the other hand a few new EU competences were introduced (such as services of general economic interest) (Mayer 2004).

Complicating the executive

The system of checks and balances at EU level is much more complex than similar systems elsewhere (such as the equivalent US system or other federal systems) because legislative, executive and judicial roles are shared among the major institutions in an atypical way that reflects the EU's particularities as a Union of peoples and member states, both of which are to be represented at the 'federal' level. The Convention did not deliberate openly on institutions as this was a contentious issue – particularly the question of where the locus of executive power would lie. The Union had several bodies exercising executive roles before the Convention: mainly the European Council, the Council of Ministers, the Council presidency and the European Commission (Westlake and Galloway 2004: 10). The division of labour among these bodies has not always been clear, and part of the exercise might have been to clarify roles and strengthen the executive as a whole. In the Convention, however, the main players focused on the question of the balance of power among the institutions that exercised and would be exercising executive functions (Craig 2004).

It may well be argued that the European Council – that is, the bi-annual meeting of the heads of state and government of the European Union acting in unanimity – represents the political will of the member states at the highest level. A proposal put forward in the Constitutional Treaty was that a long-term European Council president, appointed by the European Council itself would be needed to provide the necessary leadership, continuity and coherence for the European Council's work. The president would be an accomplished statesperson who would command general respect, but would not be a prime minister or president currently in office. The Lisbon Treaty confirmed the office. This move, among others, was designed to address the question of identifiability in matters concerning responsibility for leading the Union (Blavoukos *et al.* 2007).

Several issues can be raised at this point. First, there is the major question regarding the clarity of the division of labour between the respective roles of European Council president and Commission president. Both the European Council and the Commission *de facto* play a part in setting the agenda and defining the strategic orientations of the European Union. This is now being formalised. It is envisaged that the European Council president will set the strategic orientations and the Commission president will retain the right to initiate the multi-annual agenda, with a view to ensuring inter-institutional agreement. Paul Craig argues that, even though there is a lack of clarity regarding this division of roles, there are good reasons to expect that the two offices are more likely to co-operate than clash, because clashes will lead to inactivity and deadlock, which will be blamed on both (Craig 2004).

Secondly, the internal organisation of the European Commission is becoming more complex. In view of EU enlargement, the Draft Constitutional Treaty proposed to transform the Commission (as of 2009) into a more compact body of 13 voting Commissioners plus its president and the Foreign Minister, selected on the basis of equal rotation among member states. The College would be supported by 'non-voting' Commissioners from all other member states that would hold portfolios and attend College meetings. This has been criticised as a confusing arrangement that, in terms of clarity and simplicity, is a step back from the one-Commissioner-per-member-state principle currently at work. The Commission itself proposed that all Commissioners should vote and instead could form groups to handle more broadly defined policy areas.

A third point concerns the respective roles of the presidencies of the European Council and the formations of the Council of Ministers. After the 2004 Rome Inter-Governmental Conference (IGC) it was envisaged that Council formations would be chaired by team presidencies of three member states, held on a principle of rotation for 18 months. During that period, each of the three member states would take turns in chairing the General Affairs

Council, all Council formations other than the Foreign Affairs Council (whose make-up would be decided by the European Council) and the Committee of Permanent Representatives (COREPER) for six months. The GAC chair would act in liaison with the European Council president and the president of the Commission to ensure follow up of the European Council decisions and co-ordinate follow-up across the other Council formations. A strong European Council presidency would then be added to co-ordinate and direct the Council's rotating team presidencies towards the priorities of the European Council. The more complicated relationship and structure of roles emerging with respect to the previous regime of six-monthly rotating presidencies, can be thought of as a result of compromise between small member states that felt threatened by the strong European Council presidency (which they considered to strengthen the hand of larger member states) and the larger member states.

A fourth point concerns the office of High Representative. The holder of this post will be appointed by the European Council, will chair the Foreign Affairs Council and will be vice-president of the Commission. Their tasks will include co-ordinating and fleshing out the policy guidelines of the European Council for the CFSP and co-ordinating all aspects of the Union's external action. The post was established in part to clarify responsibilities in the Union's external representation that were not clearly delineated at the outset between the High Representative and the Commissioner for External Affairs (Cameron and Spence 2004), but it is not certain that clarification has been achieved. Quite apart from the question of the clear definition of responsibilities that the High Representative will shoulder within the Union structure of governance, a question can be raised regarding the confusion that results from the Union's three-headed representation with respect to third parties.

Are reforms in the executive branch of Union governance likely to result in clearer leadership and greater clarity and simplicity for the Union's structures? Given the complexity, and therefore reduced understandability, of the double-headed executive, the greater complexity of the internal structures of the European Commission, the fact that the presidencies of the various configurations of the Council of Ministers will no longer coincide with the presidency of the European Council, and the fact that a second new figure in the form of the EU High Representative has been added to the ranks of leading figures representing the European Union abroad, it might just be the case that the new arrangements will have exactly the opposite effects from those intended: greater complexity and diminished identifiability.

Simplifying law-making

Despite adding to the complexity of the executive, the Constitutional Treaty refrained from adding to the complexity of the legislature. By extending the application of the co-decision procedure to significant policy areas such as agriculture, the structural funds and asylum and immigration, and by making it the standard law-making procedure in the Union (with the notable exceptions of the CFSP, taxation, legal immigration and Treaty revision), the respective legislative roles of EP and Council became clearer.

Furthermore, a special Convention Working Group on Legal Simplification (chaired by Giuliano Amato, one of the Convention's vice-presidents) had the special task of dealing with the simplification of law and law-making. The working group took pains to simplify decision-making procedures and legislative acts by reducing their number and proposed the establishment of a hierarchy of norms which provides for a distinction between legislative and executive acts (Convention 2002).

Finally, the Convention also rejected all solutions that involved setting up new parliamentary bodies. Two examples can be given here. Convention president Valéry Giscard d'Estaing proposed the establishment of a 'Congress of the Peoples of Europe', a joint assembly of MEPs and national parliamentarians meeting annually, which would – among other things – nominate or confirm candidates for top EU appointments, such as the Commission's president and the permanent president of the European Council. Giscard's Congress would be consulted on the eventual evolution of Union competences as well as on eventual future enlargements and it would receive and discuss an annual report of the President of the Council and the President of the Commission on the state of the Union. Another rejected proposal was one supported by British prime minister Tony Blair which involved setting up a new body of national parliamentarians at the EU level as a second chamber of the directly elected EP (Blair 2000). Both proposals involved losses of power for the EP and therefore invited its opposition (Judge and Earnshaw 2003: 303–6). In the first case the Parliament would lose its prerogative to elect the Commission president and in the second case its role as co-legislator would be diminished; arguably both would also have resulted in less clarity and simplicity for the Union's structure.

On the other hand, some proposals designed to simplify the legislative role of the Council were rejected or scheduled to come into force only several years later. The proposal to set up a separate Legislative Council that would deal with all Union legislation, thus separating the Council's legislative role from its executive role, partly made it through the Convention, but after serious objections were raised from the member states it was discarded in the 2004 Rome IGC. Furthermore, the simplification of QMV in the Council, which involved abolishing weighed voting and shifting to a double majority system (a 55 per cent majority of member states representing at least 65 per cent of the Union's population) barely made it past the Rome IGC after Poland and Spain raised objections, and seems set to be postponed until 2014 according to the provisions of the Lisbon Treaty, largely on account of Polish objections. The current system, which was established in Nice (2001) for a Union of 25 as a temporary settlement, involves a 'triple' majority comprising a majority of weighed votes (232 out of 321), a majority of members of the Council (13 out of 25) and a majority of members of the Council representing at least 62 per cent of the Union's population (if verification is requested) (Westlake and Galloway 2004: 233–55).

The simplicity and clarity of EU governance in general, whether it leads to legislation or not, raises further concerns. First, there is a multitude of governance modes, each with its variations. In 2002, Scott and Trubek identified no fewer than six different modes of governance apart from the classical community method (CM) itself. Three of these they considered to be variations of CM: CM with greater use of framework directives, extended use of comitology, and increasing civil society involvement in the policy-making process. The other three they considered to be radical departures from CM: partnership, social dialogue and the open method of co-ordination (Scott and Trubek 2002). If we add intergovernmental decision-making in the CFSP, monetary policy decision-making by the ECB and the variations of open co-ordination resulting from its application to different policy areas (Laffan and Shaw 2005), we arrive at an unmanageable picture from the point of view of clarity and simplicity.

Furthermore, the multi-level and 'network' aspects of the EU also take their toll on simplicity. Governance practices may well have other advantages, but they certainly do not do much for simplicity. Networking in the EU involves other actors besides the main institutional actors, operating at multiple levels in the process of governance: experts, media, regional, national and European administrators, interest groups and non-governmental organisations (NGOs), and, of course, comitology. Within this network (or networks) of governance, it is not easy to discern who does what, when and how. If anything, this does not reflect a simple and clear structure of political roles and this is ultimately particularly detrimental to accountability (Peters and Pierre 2004; Papadopoulos 2007). Apart from the steps taken in legislative decision-making, the Constitutional Treaty fails to address this reality. However, positive developments may be in store in the field of comitology.

Comitology

In a narrow sense, the term 'comitology' refers to the set of advisory, management and regulatory committees whose core membership consists of member state representatives. The purpose of these committees is to advise or supervise the Commission on the implementation of duties delegated to it by the Council, and their role, in certain cases, can be decisive for the final outcome of the governmental process, although there is no significant position cut out for them in the Treaties. Committees differ according to the binding nature of consultation, their legal basis and their functions (Vos 1999: 21–22). Briefly, advisory committees can only advise the Commission, management committees can block the decisions of the Commission by a qualified majority, and regulatory committees must approve Commission decisions by qualified majority (Pedler and Bradley 2006: 243–5). Comitology is present everywhere, 'from the minutiae of technical regulation to the fundamental issues facing the Union in the present and in the future' (Christiansen and Kirchner 2000: 8).

The comitology has in the past been vast in numbers. In 1995, the Parliament asked the Commission to provide a list of all the committees and their decisions. The Commission prepared and sent to the Parliament a 2000-page, two-volume document, which listed the committees and the decisions required – not their substantive contents – for that year alone (Joerges 1999: 327–8). Since then there have been pressures to reduce the number of committees, simplify procedures and introduce greater transparency, which have borne fruit. The Commission now publishes comitology committee membership on its web site, reports to the EP on the work of committees and forwards to it all draft implementing measures (Curtin 2007: 533–4).

It is not always clear who can become a member of comitology; there are not always objective criteria that the membership of committees is required to fulfil. The members of committees are for the most part independent scientists or member state officials or representatives of interest groups called to be present on an issue-specific basis when the need arises. It is also not always clear what the tasks of each committee are or where the demarcations lie between the role of one committee and that of another. The tasks that committees are supposed to perform are by no means clearly or strictly delineated; with respect to scientific committees, for example, there is often confusion about the extent to which their role is technical and that to which it is political (Wessels 1999: 264).

The comitology is characterised by the diversity of procedures and variants of procedures followed (Vos 1999: 42–4). There are no clear-cut criteria according to which an appropriate procedure is chosen; nor is it clear who chooses the procedure to be followed and according to which rules (Azzi 1999: 53). The choice of procedure is often a matter of contestation between Council, Commission and Parliament. The Council favours so-called 'restrictive' comitology (the management and regulatory procedures) and pushes for it whenever it can; the Commission and the Parliament favour the less restrictive type of procedure (advisory procedure) (Docksey and Williams 1997: 143–50). The final choice seems often to be the result of a power struggle rather than the result of a previously settled and explicit agreement on which procedure is chosen for which issues (or categories of issues) or circumstances.

Efforts to explain the development of comitology have been made from a comparative perspective. Dehousse has pointed out that, seen from the point of view of efficiency, comitology was a 'natural' development; the EU, as a system of two-tiered government which opts for 'decentralised implementation of rules adopted at central level', has presented the tendency to develop the same type of structures, as was the case in Canada with 'executive federalism' and in Germany with 'Politikverflechtung' (Dehousse 1999:

111). Furthermore, comitology is alleged to be yet another manifestation of the growing trend towards network governance. Vos describes comitology as 'a bridge between the horizontal and vertical distribution of powers between Community and national levels, thus developing multi-level policy-making' (Vos 1999: 33). Finally, the proliferation of comitology is attributed to the fact that there is no hierarchical control over the decision-making process as a whole, which means that there is an increased and increasing need for co-operation among the institutions (Christiansen and Kirchner, 2000: 2–4)

In terms of the clarity and simplicity of law-making, the Union pays a high price for comitology, not only because it is unclear and complex with respect to its internal operation but also because it complicates the relations between the main Institutions in that context (Harlow 2002: 33). Comitology, understood as an inappropriate check of the Council on the Commission, is argued to interfere with the Commission's right of initiative and consequently with the EP's right of control (Bradley 1999).

The establishment of the category of delegated legislation, envisaged in the Constitutional Treaty was originally meant to address this question. Non-legislative acts can be issued by the Commission for the implementation of legislative acts in member states. They may not concern the essentials, but only the technical details of implementation. The EP or the Council may revoke the delegation, or the delegated legislation may come into effect only if neither of the two legislative bodies of the Union expresses objections within a time frame set in the law or framework law.

Whereas in the previous regime the Commission received regular input from member states on implementing (secondary) legislation with no *ex post* control, it is now meant to make its own choices on serious matters of a regulatory nature with *ex ante* control, which is argued to be largely ineffective. There have been criticisms that this will not represent an adequate check on the Commission (Craig 2004). On the other hand, this regime is meant to pave the way for the dismantling of comitology, particularly regulatory and management committees, and thus to simplification and greater clarity in Union law-making and implementation.

Norms supportive of identifiability

With regard to the norm of *adherence* to role-related tasks, it seems that whenever EU Institutions have had the opportunity to expand their powers, roles and influence, that opportunity has certainly been taken up. The European Commission has consistently used its right of initiative to extend Union competences and therefore strengthen its own role in the process, while the EP's constant power gains are largely a result of its own activism in asserting and expanding its role as democratic watchdog of the Union. The European Council, the Council and the member states, great and small, and more recently, national parliaments and autonomous regions, are also asserting and attempting to strengthen their roles in European governance, often at the expense of the roles of the supranational institutions of the Union.

It may certainly be necessary or desirable to bring about some changes to our role – given the modality of European Integration so far, which has involved continuous task expansion – and likewise to strengthen the institutions meant to exercise the new tasks. Yet, as we come closer to a constitutional arrangement, a new culture of self-restraint is becoming necessary, such as is to be found in the constitutional culture of federations (Craig 2004).

The weakness of the norm of taking responsibility for one's role-related tasks, which became obvious in the Santer Commission's resignation episode (Arnull 2002: 2–3), is not confined to the incumbents of the Union's political posts. It extends to the administration where often the confines between technical and political roles are unclear and officials fail to take political responsibility while acting politically (Wessels 1999: 262–4). But while it may be argued that the administration's *de facto* discretion to act politically while hiding behind administrative roles represents a problem in national contexts no less than in the EU context, this is not the case when it comes to national politicians taking responsibility for their national role-related tasks. The problem at EU level is much more serious than it is at national level.

Leadership, which by and large involves taking responsibility, is *de facto* assumed by the heads of government of the large 'older' member states at EU level – mainly France and Germany – and to a much lesser extent by the president of the Commission and the Council presidency. In the absence of an EU leader, the 'Franco-German axis' has played this role at length. Providing for one single EU leader with increased legitimacy in the Constitutional or Lisbon Treaties would have helped from the point of view of encouraging the assumption of leadership. Unfortunately, the new arrangements, which add a European Council president and a High Representative to the office of Commission president and therefore involve a system of multiple leadership for the executive, can hardly be said to promote this development.

To some extent, at the political level, the lack of senior figures recognisable by public opinion across member states who would feel compelled to take responsibility can be attributed to the diversity of languages, nations and fragmented public spaces within the EU. It can also be attributed to the fact that rewards and punishments in the EU are allocated not at European, but principally at national level by governments and political parties. It may generally be thought that this has to do with the fact that their community of reference is not Europe but their national community.

Moreover, it has widely been argued that both in the context of what concerns the CM and the open method of co-ordination, member state governments often do not take their share of the blame, shifting it to the EU. In matters concerning painful adjustments related to the introduction of the euro, fiscal restraint, labour market, pensions, educational and other reforms, member state governments have often used the Union as *vincolo esterno* (Dyson and Featherstone 1996) or engaged in 'two-level games' (Büchs 2008).

Conclusion

Identifiability, the set of properties of a system of governance which allows for the identification of responsibility, constitutes a necessary support for the practice of accountability. Identifiability has been shown to consist of institutional provisions for the clarity, stability and simplicity of the structure of political roles and binding norms dictating that political agents keep to their roles and take responsibility for their designated role-related tasks. In the EU context, serious shortcomings of identifiability have been pointed out in this chapter. Recent attempts to reform the ground rules setting out and clarifying the relationships between political roles, mainly to be found in the Constitutional Treaty, have not been crowned with success. Some progress has been achieved in what concerns the stability of political roles. Yet, with respect to the simplicity of the system of roles, new problems have emerged, which may become particularly pronounced since further complexity has been added to the make-up of the Union's executive. Finally, the atrophic development of the norms of identifiability is far from having been addressed.

5

Openness

Introduction

Identifiability enables us to locate responsibility for political outcomes and thereby makes the operation of the practice of accountability possible, otherwise we would not be able to hold agents to account. But a system of governance has another feature whose absence or failure makes accountability impossible: openness. Without information about the workings of the process of governance, political agents cannot form judgements about political responsibility; they cannot understand why a political agent is responsible, and they cannot form an opinion about why that particular political agent should – or should not – be held to account, by whom and for what. The mechanism of openness, in other words, is designed to ensure that political agents have enough information to make political judgements, and therefore, to be able to play their part in the practice of accountability (Dyrberg 2002: 83).

This chapter will first explore the relationship between openness and what it is meant to foster: political judgement. Then it will examine the limits of openness: whether all information relevant to the formation of political judgement should always be made available, or whether there are situations in which limitations are called for. Next, it will explore the institutional requirements that must be met if the mechanism of openness is to be effective; reference will be made to the presumption of openness and the establishment of exceptions, as well as to provisions for transparency. Finally, the EU system of governance will be examined from the point of view of openness and transparency.

Openness and political judgement

The idea that openness in governance generally promotes political judgement among the citizenry can be traced back to the Utilitarians: Jeremy Bentham, James and John Stuart Mill. In his 'Essay on Political Tactics', before he begins to discuss the ideal institutional organisation of assemblies, Bentham states a 'law' to which he gives the status of a first organising principle:

> the fittest law for securing the public confidence, and causing it [the Assembly] constantly to advance towards the end of its institution. This law is that of publicity. (Bentham 1962: 310)

Bentham lists four reasons in favour of publicity in assemblies and four reasons against, and argues in favour. The reasons in favour are: first, that publicity is the most constant and 'universal' way of ensuring that the members of the Assembly do their duty; second, that it alone secures 'the confidence of the people and their assent to the measures of the legislature' (Bentham, 1962: 311); third, that it allows the governed to have an enlightened opinion and, consequently, both to give the 'right' feedback to those who govern and to be in a better position in choosing their representatives; and fourth, it is more 'amusing' and therefore more conducive to the happiness of the nation. Openness then keeps the members of the Assembly accountable; it serves representation and promotes enlightened political judgement, not to mention putting a smile on the people's faces.

Bentham's objections to publicity are related, first, to the general incompetence of the public (on account of ignorance and 'passions') in making correct judgements of the proceedings in Assembly; second, to the risk that a member of the body might be exposed unfairly to public hatred; third, to the danger that demagoguery might be encouraged as a result of providing the members with such a powerful forum; and fourth, to the danger that the monarch's knowledge (in Bentham's time) of the positions of particular persons might inhibit their freedom of decision. Bentham argued that the second and third objections were reducible to the first (that the general public is not competent to make political judgements) and that this first objection fails on the grounds that since the people will judge anyway, whether or not publicity prevails, it is better that they should be given the means to judge correctly. As for the final objection, Bentham argues that the only protection that the members of Assembly can have from the sovereign comes from the people.

Moreover, for Bentham, the arguments in favour of publicity are not limited to the working of assemblies:

> The efficacy of this great instrument [publicity] extends to everything – legislation, administration, judicature. Without publicity, no good is permanent; under the auspices of publicity, no evil can continue. (Bentham 1962: 314)

For J. S. Mill, openness as uninhibited public debate allows for the pursuit of truth as a collective enterprise under conditions of fallibility (Mill [1861]: 20–61). Such, for Mill (as he sets it out in the first chapters of his *Considerations on Representative Government*), is the required ground for the operation of the educative, or 'developmental' function of politics – that is, the role that active political participation as such plays in the moral and political development of the people. Mill's concern is with the shaping of political institutions that promote the 'active' character. Within this framework, Mill went so far as to argue that voting should be open. He claimed that the dangers of secret voting – that is, voting according to self-interested concerns without any regard for the public interest and being able to get away with it, thereby causing a general decline in terms of responsibility through anonymity and concealed choice – were much greater than the dangers believed in the past to stem from open voting (Mill [1861]: 353–63).

Brennan and Pettit categorised these dangers as bribery, blackmail and intimidation. Arguing that Mill's position about open voting is not irrelevant today and could be utilised to bring about a more involving public sphere, they advocated the view that nowadays these dangers are no longer pertinent owing to the larger size of electorates, the greater power of the rule of law, the development of pluralism and the widespread experience of the democratic ethos (Brennan and Pettit 1990: 329–32).

The common strand running through these arguments in favour of openness is that openness in governance helps to create an enlightened citizenry; a citizenry capable of informed choice and political judgement. This understanding of the link between openness and the encouragement of political judgement can, *prima facie*, support (and has supported in many cases) the argument for a general presumption of openness in the governance of democratic societies.

According to Sissela Bok, there should be a presumption in favour of openness, not in politics in general, but in the politics of a democratic society. Openness should prevail unless there is good reason against it. She mentions Sweden and the USA as examples of societies whose political systems carry this presumption in the form of Acts stating freedom of information; Britain is presented as an opposite case, where the presumption is in favour of secrecy. Although laws and statutes do not tell us everything about actual openness (different traditions, different ways of mitigating the effects of these laws in either direction) the presumption for openness should prevail if a society wants to be deemed democratic (Bok 1984: 179). Nevertheless a general presumption in favour of openness need not require that all information regarding the process of governance should always be available, or that no limitations should be imposed on openness, but that when secrecy is called for it should be justified.

Limits to openness

Secrecy has always been and continues to be part of governance, including democratic governance. There are some obvious examples. Cabinets convene *in camera*. International agreements between governments are agreed and uncomfortable compromises are struck in secret. Voting is secret in general elections, and voting among MPs in parliament is sometimes secret. The first parliaments were not open to the public; they were representative bodies, deliberating and acting on behalf of the people they represented, but they were not accountable to them and their proceedings were not open. In

England, the sessions of the House of Commons were closed to both the monarch and the people. Divisions in the House were not recorded, while only the outcome of legislative proceedings, in the form of laws and resolutions, was announced at the end (Pole 1983: 89). Secrecy was very much a part of proceedings and it constituted a privilege of the MPs. The press was not allowed access to debates or to report on proceedings. What militated in favour of these restrictions was fear of blackmail and coercion from above, and fear of ignorance and bad judgement from below.

In non-democratic forms of government, sovereigns and their advisers and ministers made decisions in secret from the masses, and sovereigns made decisions alone, often to avoid being influenced or overcome by their advisers or ministers. Information has always been censored and its flow controlled by government, whether arbitrarily or under the rule of law. Information granted to the power-holder has been kept confidential, as protection both to the provider and to the user of the information.

Historically speaking, the argument for the desirability of openness as being conducive to the formation of political judgement is made possible due to technological advances in the fifteenth century, particularly the development of the printed press and can be linked to the nineteenth and twentieth century movements for universal suffrage; the arguments that justify secrecy, on the other hand, can be seen to be part of even the earliest understandings of statesmanship and governance, where the main concern was protection of the power of the realm from internal and external threats. Furthermore, the need for openness seems related to an increasingly larger and socially embracing state whose interference must be compensated by means of accountability, whereas practices of secrecy seem well suited to the early minimal state that limited its function to providing order and security. Given the present widespread acceptance of the desirability of democratic governance, and on the presumption that the role of governance calls for tasks that often go beyond those which the minimal state was required to perform, the question to ask is: if the presumption is in favour of openness, when is secrecy justifiable?

It will be argued that there are two aims that can justify secrecy in a democratic context: the first has to do with the actual formation of political judgement. Openness does not always work in favour of the formation of political judgement; it may temporarily or permanently hinder its development. In such cases secrecy may be justified. The second has to do with the maintenance of the material possibilities of forming political judgement: if openness is a threat to the very existence of a given political community, or to the operation of its system of governance, then secrecy may be justified.

When secrecy in governance is justified

Secrecy for the promotion of political judgement

One argument in favour of secrecy, which posits that political judgement is not always best served by openness, is that advanced by J. R. Pole. In discussing the matter of openness in the first parliaments in England and the United States, Pole says:

> Most Americans have, historically, been reasonably satisfied with their constitution. Yet it is very doubtful whether they would have had the Constitution if the debates of the convention had been subject to daily comment and the views of members had been subject to the pressure of local criticism while the document was in the process of being framed. Once the instrument of government lay before them, the people through their state conventions could consider it on its merits, as a whole. But that whole represented a series of complex agreements, compromises and concessions, which could hardly have been achieved in a forum open to the country. The best open covenants are not always those that have been openly arrived at. (Pole 1983: 134)

Constitutive moments, the striking of deals that amount to constitutive moments, and deliberations and negotiations leading to such moments have, more often than not, been kept secret. This has been justified on the grounds that in such cases secrecy allows the long-term interest to prevail over short-term interests and views which take into account the greater picture to prevail over views that obscure and obstruct the greater aims. Openness in this sense may hinder, rather than promote, the development of balanced political judgement. It is certainly true that making a political judgement that refers to long-term considerations requires abstraction and detachment from the concerns of the day and the partialities that these may entail. However, Pole's argument makes strong assumptions about the capabilities of citizens on the one hand and politicians on the other hand to make political judgements when equipped with the same information; the assumption is that, for some reason, citizens are interested only in short-term issues and are unable to take the long-term view, but that, by contrast, their (often deal-striking, horse-trading, log-rolling) representatives are gifted with prudence and are able to disregard short-term benefits. These assumptions are empirically questionable and normatively controversial in a democratic context. They can hardly carry the argument in favour of secrecy.

Thomas Hobbes holds secrecy in government in high esteem, when he discusses 'counsel' in the *Leviathan*. The sovereign, according to Hobbes, must always take counsel from one person at a time, in secret; never from an assembly of men. This is because in assembly, advice is not given:

> with care of the businesse propounded, but of the applause of their motly orations. (Hobbes [1651](1985): 309)

If, then, the sovereign wants to have the advice of every man, rather than the advice of the groupings of opinion that result from parliamentary debates; if the sovereign wants to eliminate from his considerations the voices of those whose interests are (according to his judgement) contrary to the interests of the public; and if the sovereign wants to examine thoroughly reasons, veracity, probity of opinion through interruptions and objections (that is, through dialogue), as well as to save precious time for 'serious' discussion of this kind rather than superficial and 'passionate' (not detached) discussion, such as takes place in assembly, then the sovereign must conduct his deliberations and receive counsel in secret and from each man separately rather than openly in and by an assembly.

Hobbes's argument is another in favour of the idea that secrecy facilitates (rather than hinders) political judgement. His is a two-step argument: first, that openness is likely to lead to demagoguery, and second, that demagoguery does no service to the formation of political judgement. The second step of the argument may well be true: demagoguery may be detrimental not only for the judgement of the sovereign, for which Hobbes is concerned, but even more so for the judgement of political agents in a democratic society. However, the first part of the argument is questionable. It may be the case that open discussion can degenerate to demagoguery, but demagoguery can also be exposed by open discussion; in fact, open discussion may well be the only way of exposing demagoguery. Again, this argument cannot justify secrecy.

Is it then never the case that openness can impair political judgement? The arguments put forward above are not convincing; another argument may be more to the point. The absence of information is never conducive to political judgement; on the other hand, too much information could hinder it. When we need to make a judgement and we are faced with an overload of information, not all of which is relevant, our judgement can become blocked. If the information is to be useful, we need to select from it only those pieces that are relevant to the judgement we need to make. However, we may be unable to do so, either because the information is too specialised or because it is too vast, or both. Our judgement may be impaired by our lack of expertise, or we may be discouraged from making a judgement altogether by our limited time resources. In such cases, secrecy, in the sense of 'pre-selection' of information, may indeed assist judgement. Pre-selection here signifies the presentation of information in such a way that it becomes more focused and targeted, and that its salient points are highlighted. Pre-selection should not mean that the information that has not been selected should not be available to the public; rather, that on top of encompassing openness, special processes should be in place to select, popularise and actively disseminate information which is judged to facilitate political judgement.

Of course, the problem in a democratic context is to determine who will do the pre-selecting. In practice, political organisations, journalists and experts pre-select the information that is publicly disseminated. The question to ask is whether those who pre-select information will do it well and with the best interest of the public at large in mind. The risks of pre-selection are addressed through the encouragement of pluralism of the sources of pre-selected information, with better results in some cases than in others.

But if the choice is between an unlimited supply of non-usable information and multiple compendia of pre-selected information with the attendant risks involved, a democratic society would, and does, go for the latter.

Secrecy for the preservation of community and the possibility of governance

If limits to openness can sometimes be justified on the grounds that they can facilitate political judgement, they can also be justified on the grounds of preservation of the very context within which political judgement is meant to develop in the first place: if the existence of the community is at stake, or if the very operation of governance is in jeopardy, limits to openness may well be justifiable.

Practices and norms of secrecy have in the past been (and continue at present to be) justified by the evocation of 'reasons of state'; such arguments make ultimate appeal to the self-preservation of a given community where the state – as the only legitimate agent of the community as a whole – is entitled to be the keeper of information that could damage the latter. Self-preservation may here be taken to mean physical, political, economic, or even cultural self-preservation. In short, self-preservation of a community may refer to anything that fundamentally constitutes the context – physical and symbolic – within which the community is able to make sense of things and find the space to flourish.

The presuppositions here are that we can distinguish the limits of such communities more or less clearly and that the state is indeed the only or the central legitimate agent of the common interest of the community. Even if we do not question that these presuppositions still hold true to the same extent as in the past (which we would have serious reasons to do) the justification of secrecy cannot be unqualified.

Firstly, what constitutes a danger is not beyond dispute. Rather, it is the crucial question to tackle on a case by case basis. Whoever takes this decision carries a burden of great responsibility. A justification of secrecy that may be valid for the self-preservation of the community in general is not automatically a valid follow-up to a decision that something in particular is dangerous. The latter needs to be argued for. We generally agree with Bok when she proposes that, in democracies, choice about secrecy should be public. She advocates that discussions about whether or not a practice or information on a particular issue should be secret ought always to be held openly (Bok 1984: 112). Democratic communities should be able to make their own trade-offs between a greater degree of insecurity and a greater degree of free-flowing information that facilitates democratic debate (Rourke 1961: 225–6).

Secondly, another aspect not covered by the general justification of secrecy on grounds of reasons of state is the duration of secrecy. Justification of secrecy applies only for as long as the relevant information constitutes a danger for the self-preservation of the community. To extend the justification of secrecy beyond this point is not automatic; it again needs to be argued for.

Apart from the preservation of a given political community, provided that the qualifications that we have advanced are respected, there is another aim that can justify secrecy: the very possibility of operating a system of governance. One argument in defence of secrecy on this count concerns political negotiations: when these are in order – as, for example, in cases of international negotiations – secrecy among negotiators is justified because in conditions of openness bargaining tools are absent (Bok 1984: 182–3). Bok points out that in a situation of 'war of all against all' (such as may be considered the conditions of unstructured international negotiation), the nation-states, as the only effective international actors, are justified in maintaining secret their strong cards, their bargaining strategies and the bottom line below which they are unwilling to go, because the promotion of their vital interests and their very survival on the international stage depends upon this secrecy. It is presumed that negotiation does actually take place in an unstructured environment, and also that states are able to keep crucial information from each other. Such assumptions do not apply internally in the EU, where negotiations are heavily structured, circumscribed by a significant load of previous commitments and conducted with the certainty that today's partners in negotiations will also be tomorrow's partners. Yet, to some extent, they may apply externally, towards third parties.

Another argument that could justify secrecy on the grounds that it is better for the efficiency of governance is that advanced by Bok with regard to the deliberations conducted in the internal operation of the administrative policy-making apparatus of contemporary governance. Bok argues that, with respect to administration, secrecy can be justified when it is meant to protect plans in the making which need time to mature and to be worked out thoroughly without external impediments.

> Secrecy for plans is needed, not only to protect their formulation, but also to develop them, perhaps to change them, at times to execute them, even to give them up ... Secrecy guards projects that require creativity and prolonged work: the tentative and the fragile, unfinished tasks. (Bok 1984: 23)

Bok advocates the idea that policy-making must be seen as a process similar to novel-writing. Writers often do not want their drafts, sketches and revisions to be seen by the wider public; they want the reader to see only the final result, polished and ready, when they are in a position to propose and defend it as a whole. With policy-making, the desideratum that justifies secrecy is the quality and completeness of governmental plans and the time needed for the formulation of arguments in their favour on behalf of their producer or producers. The problem here is that designing policy is not like isolating oneself in a room and writing a novel. In designing policy, one must take into account many things that cannot be found in a library or within the confines of a room: feedback from sources that indicate whether one or the other proposal would be acceptable or not, both by the executive and from the citizens; feedback from previous policy rounds; and so on. A policy plan proceeds by trial and error and adjusts; it is never a finished product in the sense that a novel may be. Shutting out criticism and feedback, or limiting their sources to those chosen by the person who deliberates, may lead to mistakes and prejudices that, through free flowing debate, could be avoided (Bok 1984: 25).

Finally, secrecy of deliberations conducted in the context of governance processes that are crucial for arriving at a decision are sometimes argued to be justified because publicity might lead to deadlock (Bok 1984: 182–3). There are two elements to this argument. One is time: it takes time to make all things public, to deal with objections and to give explanations to the public when, at the same time, deliberations are taking place. It takes time to let the public into those deliberations and to take it through them step by step while waiting for their approval and respecting their disapproval. When time is important because a situation is urgent and crucial problems cannot wait, openness can be an impediment.

A second element is efficiency: by opening up deliberations, at times there may be no results at all. This is because not everything can be 'legitimately' discussed in public. Deliberations sometimes entail compromises and trade-offs. These are practices that the general public allegedly is unwilling or unable to accept. Citizens here are assumed to be uncompromising purists, unable to understand the necessity of trade-offs, even if the latter were to be persuasively demonstrated to them. Trade-offs may entail a choice between two desirable options, neither of which citizens may want to give up; compromises may be such that citizens might feel that their interests are being sold short. Representatives are assumed to be somehow more capable of arriving at optimal trade-offs than citizens.

Apart from the fact that in democratic societies the burden of proof for such secrecy lies with those who make the claim that openness would lead to the impossibility of governance, these assumptions can be questionable, and the danger is that though secrecy in deliberation may make governance possible, it may at the same time debilitate the judgement of citizens. Even where secrecy in deliberations can be argued to be justifiable for reasons of time-constraints and efficiency in governance, democratic choice must place limits on secrecy. There should be no secrecy about the fact that there are deliberations going on; about the identity of the parties in the deliberations; or about the terms of the settlement agreed upon (Bok 1984: 186–7).

It has been argued that openness in democratic governance should prevail because openness facilitates political judgement, unless good reasons exist for which secrecy should be allowed to prevail. The ultimate justification for allowing practices of secrecy in the context of a democratic society is either the facilitating of political judgement or the preservation of the context within which this judgement is meant to develop. A form of secrecy, dubbed pre-selection of information, was argued to enable judgement, rather than disable it. Furthermore, it was found that a qualified version of the justification of secrecy evoking reasons of state can indeed be shown to conform to the second standard – that is, the preservation of the context within which political judgement must take place. The arguments in favour of secrecy in deliberation may be important in preserving the very possibility of governance seen as operating under limitations of time and efficiency, but they might work against facilitating the political judgement of citizens. The trade-off in such situations will have to be made on a case-by-case basis.

The institutional requirements of openness

Following on from the discussion of the basic rationale of openness is an examination of the institutional requirements that a system of governance must meet if openness is to be effective. Failure to meet these requirements means failure of openness.

Presumption of openness and justifiable exceptions

It was already discussed that there must be a presumption of openness in the operation of a democratic system of governance. This could take the form of a general statement of principle, an Act, or even an informal set of norms established through practice. That a formal statement is codified does not necessarily mean that norms of openness are operative; similarly, informal norms could be binding even if there is no formal statement of principle.

Which kind of information should the presumption of openness apply to? A useful distinction has been made by T. Tant. 'Freedom of information' has to do with individuals' access to information which regards their civil and personal freedom, such as their own school, medical or service records. 'Open government', on the other hand, has to do with government and governmental processes and requires the willingness of the government to be as open as possible about these matters. When government withholds such information, it debilitates the political judgement of citizens (Tant 1988: 18). In our discussion of openness, it is the second category of information that is relevant (the information related to 'open government') and that the presumption of openness should cover, since it is the latter that allows for the formation of political judgement.

In seeking to discover what kind of information about government and governmental processes facilitates political judgement, we cannot expect to be entitled to enter politicians' minds or bedrooms in order to dig out their innermost thoughts and speculations. We can expect first of all to have access to the documents that governments produce in the decision-making process (Robertson 1982: 180–1): minutes of meetings, vote divisions, rationales for voting one way or the other, agendas, preparatory documents, summaries of deliberations leading to decision-making and the outcomes of the decision-making process.

Access to information can be as important for openness as the availability of the information itself. An important factor is *timing*: information regarding the issues to be discussed and decided upon, as well as the elements needed in order to make a preliminary judgement on the relevant issues, must be available to interested parties and the public at an appropriate time. Another important factor is the mode of *access*: it makes a difference whether public information is actively disseminated, simply made available for any interested citizen (for example, on the Internet), or made available only upon request to the relevant authorities. Furthermore, the *form* in which information is made available is important: information should not be codified in the wrong language, written in too technical a language, or made available through media that only a minority can make use of.

The presumption of openness should be complemented by its pre-established exceptions or by guarantees that secrecy should always be justified according to the pre-established exceptions to the presumption of openness. It is not enough if any pre-established exceptions to the presumption of openness are instituted; they must also be justifiable on the grounds that were discussed earlier. Pre-selection of information, negotiations the open access to which would block the possibility of governance altogether, and our qualified version of 'reasons of state' would have to be the acceptable exceptions to the general presumption of openness.

Transparency

Openness is closely related to *transparency*, without being identical to it. Transparency grows in importance as decision-making becomes increasingly complex in the context of governance.

> although the general public receives a lot of information about how the government operates, it is still hard for individuals to understand how the decisions are actually made since the decision-making process is so complex. (Larsson 1998: 40)

Transparency is about being able to trace the 'history' of a decision throughout the decision-making process, from proposal to implemented action. It is about being able to see 'how a particular standard was adopted, and who was involved in the decision according to a certain set of standard operating procedures' (Weale, 2000b: 167). Under conditions of complexity the availability of information *per se* becomes as important as the availability of information about governance processes and the conditions for making the information available in the context of such processes. It is therefore a requirement of transparency that information about the governmental process is available and understandable (which process, under which rules, which actors were involved) and that a decision, act or proposal can be traced back to its source.

Furthermore, it is important to note that transparency may be a property of a system of governance from the point of view of the expert few (officials, politicians, specialised journalists, organised civil society, interest groups), but not from the point of view of citizens at large. In other words, transparency may allow interested and informed parties to follow complex procedures when those interested are already familiar with these complex procedures. Under these circumstances, simplicity of governance procedures becomes an imperative if citizens at large are to be able to make use of transparency provisions in order to form political judgement.

Openness in the EU

Several objections can be raised concerning the present state of affairs in the EU from the point of view of openness. Although a presumption of openness and a catalogue of justified exceptions are now in force, doubts can be raised about the content and scope of these exceptions, particularly in what concerns the leeway for secrecy in deliberations and negotiations allowed for the Union's executive – that is, the Commission and the Council and the secrecy surrounding information protected on grounds of 'the public interest'. Furthermore, active dissemination of relevant information as opposed to passive general availability of information is yet at an embryonic state. Furthermore, it should be seen how transparent different decision-making processes are in the EU. The CM, the ECB's monetary policy decision-making, inter-governmentalism and the open method of co-ordination will be examined.

Presumption of openness and exceptions

It is not breaking the news to say that the issue of openness has, in recent times, been controversial in the EU. The negative first result of the Danish referendum on the adoption of the Maastricht Treaty (Treaty on European Union 1992) and the French result, which was a yes but a very marginal one, produced turmoil among the European governmental elites and brought the issues of openness and transparency to the fore of the European debate in the early 1990s. It became noted that the EU was too distant from the citizens whose common freedoms and citizenship status it had recently acknowledged. Subsidiarity and transparency became key words and were addressed as the panacea that would resolve the perceived democratic deficit (Lodge 1994: 244–7). The expansion of the co-decision procedure, the accession of the Scandinavian countries and the cumulative effects of low turnouts in European parliamentary elections later pushed in the same direction (Heyes-Renshaw and Wallace 1997).

Transparency became a key part of the inter-institutional discourse in the period between the signing of the Maastricht Treaty in 1992 and the signing of the Amsterdam Treaty in 1996 (Treaty of Amsterdam 1997), when the first steps on the issue of openness were made. These included the 1993 Inter-Institutional agreement, which provided a first approach to the right of access to documents and exceptions (Public Access to the Institutions' Documents 1993), the adoption of new rules for drafting Community legislation in order to make it more accessible (Resolution on the Drafting of Community Legislation 1993) and the changes in the 1993 Council's Rules of Procedure, which allowed for public debates and publication of votes and minutes when the Council acts in legislative mode (Council of the European Union 1993). In those early years of opening up, the first televised Council debates took place, which were, however, 'in fact not real debates, but rather monotonous monologues of ministers reading out speeches prepared before the meeting' (Bauer 2004: 327). With regard to the other institutions of the Union, it was the imperative of the European Ombudsman's first report to the EP that all institutions should establish and publish the procedures according to which access to the information they handled would be organised. The response was positive (The European Ombudsman 1998: C 44/9).

In the Preamble of the Amsterdam Treaty it was stated that the Treaty 'marks a new stage in the process of creating an ever closer union among the peoples of Europe, in which decisions are taken as openly as possible and as closely as possible to the citizen' (Treaty of Amsterdam 1997: Article 1). Article 255 called upon EU Institutions to implement 'transparency' provisions by 1 May 2001, hence Regulation 1049/2001 regarding public access to EP, Council and Commission documents was adopted. The aim of Regulation 1049/2001 is to give the 'fullest possible effect to the right of access to the institutions' documents and to establish general principles and limits to such access', as well as to establish rules regarding the facilitation of the exercise of that right and set out good relevant administrative practice (European Parliament and Council 2001).

The presumption of openness and the grounds for justifiable exceptions are stated in paragraph 11 of the introductory section: 'In principle all documents of the institutions should be accessible to the public. However, certain public and private interests should be protected by way of exceptions'. 'Public interest' denotes 'public security, defence and military matters, international relations and the financial, monetary or economic policy of the Community or a Member State' (Article 4§1). Limits related to private interests concern the protection of the privacy and integrity of the individual. Areas excluded are those concerning commercial interests, court proceedings and legal advice, as well as the purpose of inspections, investigations and audits (Article 4§2).

The right of access also applies to documents related to the CFSP and police and judicial co-operation in criminal matters with respect to the rules of security of each institution. Documents regarding public security, defence and military matters are to be considered as 'highly sensitive' documents, which should be given 'special treatment' with regard to public access. Such documents will be released only if the institution in question consents. They will be handled only by authorised persons that will also assess which references can be made to those documents in the public registers. Each institution will publicise its own rules regarding access to sensitive documents. Refusal will be justified, but in a way that will not harm the security interests involved. The Commission and Council will inform the EP about sensitive documents, according to arrangements made between the institutions (Article 9).

Any EU citizen or any other entity with legal personality may request any document issued by or in possession of an EU Institution, subject to the above restrictions. Institutions on their part are under the obligation to respond to requests for documents within fifteen days and to provide justification for potential refusals.

We are concerned here with open government rather than freedom of information, so it is the question of public interests that must be dealt with. As argued above, 'reasons of state' referred to the protection of the community, and reasons related to the very operation of a system of governance may indeed justify secrecy and therefore provide an argument against the disclosure of certain documents. However, it must be demonstrated or argued that something does in principle constitute a threat to security or to the efficiency of governance, and this must be a matter for democratic choice. What can be seen in Regulation 1049/2001 is that such decisions are not up to democratic choice but up to the institutions to make, and the latter must therefore decide what the 'public interest' consists of.

Institutions are to provide for the widest possible access to documents when acting in their legislative capacity, yet they must respect the principle that their capacity to execute their tasks must not be compromised. According to Article 4§3, access to documents that are produced during internal deliberations or preliminary consultations or to documents that relate to a matter on which an institution has not yet made a decision may be refused if their disclosure would seriously undermine the institution's decision-making process, unless there is an overriding public interest at stake.

Again, what constitutes a threat, this time to an Institution's decision-making efficiency, is left to the institution to decide. Certainly, the institution must justify its refusal to grant access to a document and it will do so on the basis of the exceptions mentioned in Article 4. However, the application of the rule to each specific case is mostly up to the institution, without appropriate safeguards, as it is not clear exactly what would jeopardise the efficiency of decision-making and why.

In 2007 the European Commission published a Green Paper (GP) inviting consultation in order to consider needed revisions of Regulation 1049/2001. The GP provided a positive evaluation of the improvement of public access to documents, noting that all institutions had set up public registers of documents, more documents had been made directly available, and requests had multiplied. It was estimated that about two-thirds of requests for information had been granted by Council and Commission, while the EP had granted more than eighty per cent of requests for access to documents (Commission of the European Communities, GP 2007: 4). The main reasons for rejecting requests have been the effective internal operation of the EU decision-making institutions and cases where private interests would have been at stake (GP 2007: 5). In its re-evaluation of the Regulation, the GP focuses mainly on the protection of private interests from the disclosure of information and fails to address either conflicts between openness and the public interests or the decision-making secrecy of institutions.

Accessibility to information in Regulation 1049/2001 is promoted by provisions obliging each institution to set up a public register of documents on its website, and to update that register in timely fashion. These are particularly obligatory in matters concerning the legislative process, but also, insofar as possible, the policy-making process. The Union's three main institutions have responded to this requirement by providing public access to the law-making process and the *Official Journal* via the Europa server. The 2007 GP recommends that provisions should be made to extend the notion of legislative document to include the more preparatory documents and make these accessible through the Internet in the most user-friendly way possible (GP 2007: 11–12).

Furthermore, the three institutions have set up separate public registers of documents. The Commission has made its own register available on-line since 2002 and it has made the minutes of its meetings available on the Internet since January 2002. Its 'Transparency' web site also provides links for access to the register for comitology committees, the register of expert advisers and the CONNECS database, where lobbyists are listed on a voluntary basis (Commission Transparency web site). The EP is, by the nature of its proceedings but also by policy, the most open of the EU institutions. It has a mandatory system of accreditation for lobbyists, and its committees are open. It made its official register available on-line in 2002. The Council has also set up a public register of documents which contains references to documents produced from 1999 onwards; some documents can be displayed directly, while others must be requested from the Council's document access service. Since 2006, the Council has also made public its debates through video streaming in all EU languages, while a recorded version is available for at least one month on the Council's web site. Other institutions have risen to the challenge as well.

The Commission has taken initiatives to improve and simplify law-making in the EU so that it is more accessible and efficient. Yet, accessibility depends not only on making relevant information publicly available but also on actively disseminating it. Daily press releases are issued to 'popularise' the initiatives, views, decisions and policy proposals of the main institutions. But all things considered, EU law and policy remain too 'technical' for the average citizen. The potential role of the media in popularising and actively disseminating information , particularly European-level media, could not be stressed more here. Unfortunately, a lot is left to be desired on this front (Abbott 2002).

Transparency

In the case of the EU it is not only the complexity but also the multitude and diversity of decision-making processes that raise a number of serious questions from the point of view of transparency. Complexity arises from the fact that decision-making involves a multitude of actors at multiple levels. The fact that there are numerous decision-making processes in itself makes it difficult for citizens to know where to seek information and through which channels a decision and the information attached to it can be traced. Moreover, each of the main processes of decision-making presents different problems from the point of view of transparency. A distinction may be drawn between supranational decision-making, which is exemplified by the ECB's governance of monetary policy, the CM, inter-governmental decision-making, which is exemplified by the governance of the CFSP, and the different forms of policy co-ordination in the EU.

Supranational governance

The governance of the ECB is the most clearly supranational form of governance in the EU. The members of the Executive Board, the six-member body that, along with the Governing Council (including the Governors of the Eurozone Central Banks) is at the heart of the formulation and management of implementation of the EU's monetary policy, are appointed for eight-year, non-renewable terms. They are all distinguished experts in monetary matters and are selected on that criterion. They are also completely independent from member state governments. Monetary policy decisions are taken under complete secrecy, and all that outsiders are allowed to know are the final outcomes. It is thus a completely non-transparent process (McNamara 2006). This is meant to be justified in terms of the protection of the public interest, in terms of Regulation 1049/2001, or the very possibility of governance as argued in previous sections. Secrecy in the deliberations of the ECB is thought to lead to swift and efficient decision-making and to protect decision-makers from the temptation of not taking decisions that are necessary but unpopular.

As argued above, in democratic societies, closing off deliberations at preparatory stages of decision-making leads to limited input and problematic feedback from those who might want to make other contributions to a problem or question. In this case, lack of transparency in monetary policy decision-making may lead to the policy not being sufficiently informed by other economic policy priorities such as growth and employment. This raises questions about how well the public interest is in fact defended by practices of secrecy and why the bankers of the ECB are best suited to articulate, specify and implement their version of the public interest.

Community method

In those areas where the Community or Union legislates by means of the CM, three main actors contribute to the making of a decision. The European Commission has the exclusive right of initiative. In the formation of its legislative proposals the Commission consults with committees made up of national officials, experts and/or civil society organisations. The two main forms that a Commission proposal will take is regulation (or European Law as proposed in the Constitutional Treaty) or directive (Framework Law). The former, if approved, is directly and uniformly effective across the Union. The latter must be transposed in national legislation according to national circumstances as regards the institutional, legal and political system of each member state, before being brought into effect.

A Commission proposal will be sent to the EP and the Council of Ministers, the Union's two legislative bodies. Consultation, co-operation, co-decision and assent, the four major established legislative procedures, differ according to the extent to which the EP can have a decisive say with regard to the content of the final decision or the acceptance of the decision overall, or, to put it differently, according to the relative legislative power it enjoys with respect to the Council. Co-decision (largely argued to render EP and Council equal legislators) has become, particularly after the Constitutional Treaty, the default legislative procedure for the Union, with few exceptions.

The EP decides by majority while the Council decides by qualified majority, which, according to current arrangements, is in place when a majority of weighed votes (where each member state is allocated a number of votes according to the size of its population) has been mustered in favour of a proposal. After a first reading where the EP is consulted, and a second reading in which both bodies have proposed amendments that the Commission has accepted, the decision is passed. If no agreement is reached at that stage, a tripartite conciliation committee is set up to negotiate changes. If agreement is reached the decision will pass; if not, the proposal falls.

Apart from the complexity of its procedures, which leads to an objective difficulty of the layperson to follow a decision from beginning to end, the CM has traditionally had two weaknesses from the transparency point of view; these can be thought of as two blind spots in the process, which relate to what was discussed in the previous section: the secrecy involved at the stage in which the formation of the Commission's proposal takes place and the secrecy of Council deliberations when it acts in legislative mode. Steps have been taken in recent years to deal with both.

Since the beginning of the transparency debate, the Commission's main concern has been to safeguard the 'space to think' and its consultations with national politicians and interest groups at the early stages of formulating proposals. Most Council members were principally concerned with the secrecy of the negotiation process in Council, fearing that practices of openness may undermine trust between members and the effectiveness of decision-making. Among them, the great military powers of the Union have been particularly keen on protecting sensitive documents related to security and defence.

On the other hand, the EP, a defender of open democratic procedures, requires openness and transparency in the preparatory stages of decision-making in both Commission and Council committees as well as when the Council deliberates in legislative mode. This enables the EP to be a more able co-legislator, to monitor the executive more effectively and to promote citizens' rights to be informed and consulted during the decision-making process. A minority of member state governments (mainly those of the Nordic countries and Austria), coming from traditions of open government, defended the presumption of openness entailing extensive citizens' rights to access information, with few clearly defined exceptions (Bjurulf and Elgström 2004: 253–4).

In matters concerning the protection of the Commission's consultations with committees, interest groups or experts at the policy formulating stage, which the Commission considers the safeguarding of its 'right to think', progress has been made. In 2003 the Commission published its minimum standards for consultation which urges lobbyists involved in contributing to Community decision-making and policy-making to publish information on the CONNECS web site regarding the interests they represent and the inclusiveness of that representation. In December 2005, Commissioner Siim Kallas announced a Transparency Initiative, one of the three main purposes of which was to re-examine the rules under which lobbying EU institutions ought to take place, the other two being transparency regarding EU funding and strengthening the service ethic of officials employed in EU institutions. This led to the issuing of a Commission GP on Openness and Transparency in May 2006 (GP 2006).

In its GP the Commission opts for a 'soft' approach, whereby lobbyists will be given incentives to sign up to the register disclosing information on the interests they represent, their mission and their sources of funding and set up their own code of conduct, while a mechanism for monitoring and sanctions in case of breach of the code of conduct should be put in place. Mandatory registration (a version of which applies to lobbyists to the EP) was rejected, despite the view of several civil society associations that fair play and transparency demand such measures. The GP noted that if self-regulation fails compulsory registration measures will be taken (GP 2006). In his presentation of the GP, Commissioner Kallas noted that limits to openness are required if the Commission is not to turn into a 'talking shop'. He argued in favour of limits to openness, since in his view it is necessary to keep a "space for reflection" that allows policy-makers to discuss options behind closed doors in the preparatory stages of legislation (Kallas 2006).

Yet it was argued in this chapter that this is not justifiable because policy-making is not a process that can be sealed off to feedback at any stage of the decision-making process in democratic societies. Secrecy in the content of consultations and on the choice of whom to consult is a major flaw in terms of transparency. Input must be given and the provenance, terms and content of the input must be public. Knowing who says what is important because stronger parties may be unfairly heard at the expense of others.

In matters concerning the Council, measures are being taken to open up legislation by means of the rules set out in regulation 1049/2001. The will to do so became clear in the deliberations of the Constitutional Convention and was reflected in the Constitutional Treaty. According to Article I-24 §6 of the Constitutional Treaty, the 'Council shall meet in public when it deliberates and votes on a draft legislative act. To this end, each Council meeting shall be divided into two parts, dealing respectively with deliberations on Union legislative acts and non-legislative activities'. Article I-50 regarding the transparency of the proceedings of the Union's bodies reiterates the importance of debating and voting on legislation in public, both in what concerns the Council and in what concerns the EP. It also extends provisions regarding access to documents and the obligation to specify relevant provisions in their rules of procedure to all the Union's institutions, bodies, offices and agencies. As a result of pressures coming mainly from the EP, the Ombudsman and civil society organisations, the Council decided in 2005 to open up its legislative procedures.

A 2006 report submitted by to the EP by Green MEP David Hammerstein Minz leading to an EP Resolution showed the EP's concern with the continuing secrecy of the Council's legislative practices, urging it to amend its rules of procedure according to the Treaties, Regulation 1049/2001 and the principles laid out in the Constitutional Treaty. The Report pointed out that openness should extend to COREPER, which comprises representatives of member states at ambassador level, filters political decisions and presents only controversial ones to be taken by the Council. This is a political function that is not carried out openly but again under secret deliberations or negotiations, and with conciliation committees which involve the Council as co-legislator. The report also pointed out that revision of the Council's *Rules of Procedure* should include clarifications on the actual proceeding of public meetings and their content in order to avoid a shifting of real negotiations and deliberations downwards to COREPER or upwards to the European Council (Minz 2006).

In June 2006 the Council issued its new *Rules of Procedure*, with important changes to its transparency policy. These incorporate full public access to: Council deliberations on legislative acts to be adopted by co-decision, votes and the explanation of votes by Council members; Council's first deliberations on legislative acts other than those adopted by co-decision, which, in view of their importance, are presented orally by the Commission in a Council session; and the GAC's deliberations on the eighteen-month programme, spanning three presidencies. The Council is also to hold public debates regularly on important issues affecting the interests of the Union and its citizens.

It seems that the Council has largely been forced out into the open when it comes to its legislative work. However, because of a continuing fear that transparency will harm decision-making efficiency, there is the danger that if openness of deliberations in the Council of Ministers is extended to deliberations in other parts of the Council hierarchy, crucial decisions will be shifted to more informal settings, which would render the process less rather than more transparent. So far, experience has shown no significant delays or paralysis in Council decision-making caused by greater openness (Bauer 2004: 387).

Inter-governmental decision-making

In terms of transparency, inter-governmental decision-making in the EU, as exemplified by the CFSP, is less complex in the sense that it is simpler to understand a process whereby CoGs or Ministers decide on matters by unanimity after negotiations than to conceptualise the CM with its variants. However, it is much less transparent in the sense that the greatest part of the decision-making process, involving negotiations between the governments, takes place in secret.

Concerns have also been raised for secrecy in other parts of the Council hierarchy where inter-governmental decision-making takes place, involving negotiations held in secret. The European Council, the body that binds the Member States of the Union at the highest level, is composed of CoGs and takes most of the strategic decisions for the Union's general orientations. Although the European Council, in areas where the Union legislates, is not meant to be a legislative body, it acts as court of last resort for issues left unresolved at lower levels of the Council hierarchy, which at times involve compromises on the content of controversial legislation. Yet its deliberations are held behind closed doors and only the Presidency Conclusions are published, all other aspects of meetings being sealed off to the public. It is by and large the most secretive political body in the EU. It can be argued that deliberations regarding the strategic orientations of the Union may be covered by secrecy if this is convincingly argued to be useful in terms of reasons of state or safeguarding the efficiency of decision-making overall. However, at least in matters pertaining to ultimate disagreements related to legislation, European Council secrecy should not be an alibi to bypass what has been agreed for Council transparency.

Not only is the Council of Ministers one of the core legislative bodies of the Union in policy areas where co-decision and other legislative modes are used; it also takes decisions in the CFSP and co-ordinates policy in areas covered by the Lisbon agenda. Even if progress in terms of transparency is being made on the legislative front, this is not the case when it comes to the CFSP, anti-terrorism and the European Security and Defence Policy, or in areas governed through the open method of co-ordination.

In July 2000, The General Secretary of the CFSP, Javier Solana, in what became known as a 'summer coup', anticipated the new rules on access to documents that the Treaty of Amsterdam had commanded by issuing a Decision which established a system for the classification of documents with particular reference to 'military and non-military crisis management in the framework of reinforced European security and defence policy' (Council of the EU 2000a: 1). Documents judged by the Secretariat General to be sensitive for security would be classified as 'Top secret', 'Secret' or 'Confidential', they would not be mentioned in the public register and they would not be disclosed to the public for as long the Secretariat General deemed necessary. After a five-year period, however, such documents would be reviewed and, if de-classified, would be archived and subjected to the rules pertaining to non-classified documents. The rationale was that secrecy was justified under the logic that if collective security was at stake, this was equivalent to 'reasons of state'. This was expressed as harm to 'the essential interests of the Union or of one or more of its Member States' (Council of the EU 2000a: 1).

Yet, as was argued earlier in this chapter, in democratic societies, to determine what and for how long something constitutes a threat (much more so in the EU where it must be decided what is a *common* threat) must be a matter of democratic choice. This is not the case with the Common Security and Defence Policy, which, as things stand, is not subject to effective public debate and democratic decision-making at either EU or national level (Wagner 2006). In fact, the CFSP has brought about a partial transfer of foreign policy from the national level, where it was subject to open public debate, to the EU level, where it is not. Moreover, the transfer itself has often meant that certain issues are no longer debated openly at national level (Dyrberg 2002: 82–3). This was partially mitigated by the Council's Rules of Procedure (RoP) change in 2006 to the effect that the eighteen-month programme for the CFSP is to be debated in public. The extent to which these deliberations will also address security issues and the substantive policy questions involved remains to be seen. Furthermore, even where secrecy is justified for 'reasons of state', we still need to know what is being discussed, when it is being discussed, who is participating in the discussion and what the outcome is. This is not ensured by the secrecy rules surrounding security matters in the Union.

The situation with regard to openness in the Union's foreign policy is better when compared with the security component of the CFSP. The public discussion of the eighteen-month programme of the Council Presidency (over three terms) will at least provide an opportunity for open discussion of the priorities of foreign policy and the Union's role in the world, and indirectly that discussion can be thought to constitute an appropriate opportunity for the public to formulate views that can provide input for democratic choice.

Policy co-ordination

It has been widely argued in recent years that one of the greatest advantages of the new governance methods that have exploded in the EU, the most typical of which is the OMC, designed to provide a framework for decision-making in the policy areas falling under the heading of the Lisbon Strategy is that they contribute to the improvement of openness and transparency.

Rather than using top-down legal avenues to enforce policy homogeni-sation on the grounds of a European binding norm, the aim of the OMC is gradual convergence of national policies towards general guidelines that are agreed by member states meeting in the European Council, fol-lowing a Commission proposal. Member states are the core policy-makers, whereas the Commission's role is much more managerial and facilitative of co-ordination. Special committees composed of national and Commis-sion officials, the most significant of which are the Employment Committee (EMCO), the Social Protection Committee (SPC) and the Economic Policy Committee (EPC), play a significant role in setting up indicators and the day-to-day business of co-ordination. Convergence involves quantitative targets but not specific practices or institutions, which differ radically among mem-ber states. Each member state annually produces a national reform plan to show how it has moved towards agreed common EU targets and what its plans are for the following year (Chiatelli 2006).

The OMC involves soft implementation of guidelines through instru-ments such as benchmarking, peer review and exchange of best practices. Published comparative league tables showing the relative performance of member states on the grounds of specific indicators are designed to play a key role in enticing national governments to implement policy reforms through public 'naming' and 'shaming'. If national performance is found to be lagging behind by comparison with other member states, governments will be encouraged to reform through various pressures exercised towards them through peer review (by other governments), Commission recommen-dations and national opposition from parliament (Duina and Raunio 2007), as well as those of civil society and non-governmental actors. Rewards take the form of having one's national practices singled out as 'best practices' in special sessions. Openness and dissemination of information are from this point of view crucial for the effectiveness of the OMC.

Furthermore, transparency is thought to be promoted through the oppor-tunities provided by the OMC for the involvement and participation of organised civil society, national parliaments, the social partners and local government in consultations regarding the drafting of national reform plans at national level. Likewise, at EU level, the EP, the Committee of the Regions and the Economic and Social Committee, as well as EU-level civil society organisations and other actors, are consulted at the stage of drafting the Guidelines.

Although it is complex and in some respects even more difficult to follow than the CM and its variants, the OMC is thus said to promote transparency by opening up decision-making to greater consultation with civil society, the social partners and sub-national-level actors; it is said to be more open in the sense that it involves the publication of league tables, annual reform plans and policy guidelines (Hodson and Maher 2001).

Clearly, the OMC can be argued to be more open that both supranational and inter-governmental decision-making. Nonetheless, there are several ways in which it is less transparent than the CM. The OMC may be open in the sense of making information available, yet that information is highly technical, and league tables can only really be understood by specialists (Tsakatika 2004). Furthermore, the process is at least as complex as in the CM because it allows for greater policy diversity among member states. As the process is so complex that it cannot be understood by the layperson, and despite the openness involved, politicians at the national level can play 'two-level games' by shifting the blame for bad performance on to the EU (Büchs 2008).

The OMC involves intergovernmental negotiations held behind closed doors in the context of the European Council, the Council of Ministers and the special high-level Committees that facilitate day-to-day co-ordination engaging the Commission and the member states. While the Council has been forced to operate in a more transparent way in the context of legislation through the CM, this is not the case for the OMC. Open deliberations are not required when decisions on Guidelines are made in the European Council and the Council of Ministers because the obligation to deliberate in public only holds for cases where decisions on binding rules are made; guidelines are merely 'soft law'. In brief, while the OMC can be argued to promote openness, it is not as accessible or transparent as may be thought at first blush (Hodson and Maher 2001; Szyszczak 2002).

Conclusion

In this chapter it was argued that openness and transparency are prerequisites of accountability because they facilitate the formation of political judgement. The only acceptable exceptions to openness in a democratic society refer to cases where openness would harm the formation of political judgement, where it can convincingly be argued to jeopardise the very material or symbolic context within which political judgement can be formed, or where it can render governance unworkable. It was shown that in the EU considerable progress has been made in terms of openness and transparency since the early 1990s when the matter was raised. The presumption of openness has been established for documents issued by all the Union's institutions, while some exceptions could be more precisely defined and circumscribed, particularly in what concerns 'sensitive documents' referring to security matters. In terms of transparency, progress has been made concerning the 'blind spots' in the CM having to do with the Commission's 'space to think' in the preparatory stages of policy-making and Council legislative secrecy. This is not to say that we should overlook new lacunas of transparency that may result from the operation of other modes of governance, such as the OMC.

6

Conclusions

In seeking to reach a verdict for the EU's responsibility deficit, the following chapter will attempt to summarise findings and evaluate the current state of affairs by looking at three interrelated questions. First, what can we make of the current shortcomings of responsibility on the institutional side after having examined the EU from the point of view of accountability, identifiability and openness? Second, how do recent developments, and particularly the failure to ratify the Constitutional Treaty and the agreement to forge ahead with the Lisbon Treaty, affect our assessment? Finally, what might be the long-term effects of the latest developments for the deep rooted Monnet conception of legitimate 'responsible technocratic' governance?

Institutional deficits of responsibility

When it comes to accountability, the Constitutional debate that seems to be drawing to a close for the time being has left open the question of the model of checks to the executive. It has yet to be settled whether the Commission is to evolve into a political European parliamentary executive dependent on an EP majority with the Council acting as a strong second chamber, if on the contrary the Council is to evolve into an EU collective government with a long-term Council President and High Representative effectively checked by national parliaments with a Commission in the role of a qualified secretariat, or if a new *sui generis* formula for the division of labour between Commission and Council is to emerge in the context of the EU's 'power map', requiring us to rethink accountability checks.

The question of the model of checks is directly related to the question of how best to develop the forum dimension of accountability in the EU, the lack of which is arguably the weakest aspect of overall accountability in the EU. The sole presence of national (and subnational) fora is not sufficient for the forum side of accountability in the Union. On the other hand, the development of EU-level forum, at least for those issues that require a distinctively European perspective, requires practices of EU-level public and politically explicit contestation and deliberation. For that purpose, it is the model of checks incorporated in a parliamentary Commission that would be more suitable for the strengthening of the practice of accountability. It is in the context of a strong EP, enabled to nominate candidates for the Commission presidency from its own ranks or party groups, that EU level practices of contestation and deliberation can develop and enter the realm of EU-level public attention. The issue of the nomination of Commissioners would need to be thought through as well, because a partisan president would not translate into a partisan Commission (Hix 2005: 205), unless the political affiliation of Commissioners also became linked to the results of EP elections. Nonetheless, it is clear that not all issues related to the EU are exclusively EU-level issues or that they only have a European dimension. Most competences are shared between the national and the European level and therefore most issues are both European and national. A multi-level forum must therefore develop, which incorporates national and EU fora. The emergence of a multi-level forum comes up against the following obstacle: co-operative federalism and shared competence leads to executive dominance and the undermining of forum at both national and EU levels (Börzel and Risse 2000, Börzel and Sprungk 2007). In its turn, and for other reasons related to the promotion of the institutional preconditions of political responsibility, a question is raised here regarding identifiability in the EU and its relation to the cataloguing of competences.

Institutions such as the Congress of the Peoples of Europe, proposed by Valéry Giscard d'Estaing but not approved by the Convention plenary, and the establishment of practices of European Weeks and Joint Parliamentary Meetings, particularly on issues such as the Lisbon Strategy and the CFSP established after the Convention at the initiative of the EP (Tsakatika 2007b), are positive steps in this direction as they provide linkages between national and EU fora, buttress the development of EU-level forum and, at the same time, upgrade national fora.

Finally, a parliamentary Commission would make it more likely that a forum would develop at EU level that would provide the background against which the allocation of EU-level rewards and punishments in relation to the promotion or demotion from political office can take place. Yet the allocation of rewards and punishments in a multi-level forum can take a variety of forms alongside the European parliamentary route. One of these could be the naming and shaming mechanism of the OMC, though it concerns only the practices of states and regions and not political platforms. Another could be selection mechanisms developed within European parties for nominations to European offices and national offices with EU responsibilities. The latter would require reform in the way European election campaigns are run and funding rules for EU parties. A third option could be a more active opposition in national parliaments on matters with a European dimension; this would increase the possibility that the reasons for which a national government loses or wins national elections are related to performance in the EU.

Coming to identifiability, the choice of the constitutional avenue, which signifies a departure from the modality of European integration as known thus far, together with the political mechanisms established to contain 'competence creep' and manage constitutional change initially seemed likely to have a positive effect in the direction of enhancing the stability of political roles in the EU. On the other hand, the Constitutional Treaty itself brought mixed results in terms of the simplicity and clarity of the political roles embedded in the EU's institutional structure. The European Convention attempted to simplify the legislative process (and to some extent it succeeded in doing so), but inter-institutional and inter-governmental bargaining seems to have coughed up greater complexities in the executive. EU governance overall remains complex and undecipherable in terms of who does what, but we may be seeing some light at the end of the tunnel in what concerns comitology. Finally, it is clear that strengthening the identifiability of roles in the institutional structure will not be sufficient to strengthen the norms of identifiability, the development of which depends upon other factors.

Overall, the EU, more so than most established nation-states and post-national systems of governance, seems poised between the Schylla of 'many hands' and the Charybdis of 'personification'. The main source of the particularly pronounced problem of many hands in the EU is the structure of the Union's vast, plural, multi-level and network-like administrative-cum-political apparatus, in which politics is intermeshed with the technicalities of governance. To this has now been added a problem of many heads, which results from the new complexity of executive power. Personifying responsibility is thus rendered more difficult, rather than simpler in the EU.

Important steps to improve the openness aspect of the responsibility deficit have indeed been taken over the past decade and a half. The presumption of openness has by and large been established in the EU's institutions of governance. Justifiable exceptions have been established, though improvements should be considered with regard to making the application of those exceptions less dependent on the *ad hoc* decisions of the Institutions themselves; making decisions on such applications may touch upon the question of who defines the public interest and how. Likewise, institutions should have less freedom in making their own decisions on the burden that openness would place on their internal decision-making efficiency.

The question of how to define the public interest comes down to politics at the EU level: we need to allow democratic choice to be brought to bear on questions such as what constitutes a danger to European security (internal and external), what role the Union should play in the world, what trade-offs should be made between economic growth and monetary stability and between efficiency (or security) and democracy. Clearly, a great deal might be achieved by encouraging democratic contestation on matters of principle while allowing secrecy in implementation and by rethinking transparency of decision-making in the sensitive areas in such a way as to allow for rich public debate (ECB, CFSP, ESDP). Political choice and public debate would facilitate accessibility to information and its active dissemination. The atrophy of EU level communication is linked to the questions raised regarding the establishment of the multi-level fora as sketched out above, the development of a multi-level public sphere, politicisation and the role of the media.

With regard to transparency, the main problems in the EU system of governance are the following: the protection of the Commission's 'right to think'; the question of Council secrecy when it comes to COREPER and the European Council, as well as the danger that actual decision-making will be shifted to informal meetings; the secrecy that continues to surround supranational and intergovernmental decision-making; and the complexity and intergovernmental secrecy of the OMC.

The protection of the Commission's 'right to think' has been advocated on the grounds of decision-making efficiency: it is questionable to what extent decision-making efficiency would be jeopardised if processes of consultation and policy formulation were more open. Rather, it is possible that decision-making would be more efficient because it would be more widely considered legitimate and for that reason more acceptable and accepted.

With regard to the Council, the idea for a separate Legislative Council on the model of a second chamber (such as the Bundesrat) has been aired in the European Convention. It was proposed by Giuliano Amato but opposed by most national governments (Norman 2003). Such a solution would have cut the Gordian knot of the Council's exercise of both legislative and executive functions, but it was thought that it would render the Council's work difficult in terms of coining compromises. Giscard d'Estaing promoted the idea of a joint General Affairs and Legislative Council, which was intended to achieve a compromise between the two positions. However, at the October 2004 IGC in Rome, which finalised the end-product of the Constitutional Treaty, Giscard d'Estaing's position was overridden and the final document did not name a Legislative Council at all, either on its own or in conjunction with the GAC, but simply called for the Council to meet in special session on legislative matters.

Until legislative openness in the Council is fully achieved we will not know if it represents a real danger for efficient legislative decision-making, although the signs are positive so far. It will then be seen if the problem stems from a lagging and outdated culture of diplomacy and secrecy, or if it is a problem that must be resolved through institutional reform. Were the latter to be the case, reconsideration would need to be given to the separation of the Council's legislative and executive functions.

All things considered, it seems that the CM, despite its 'blind spots', seems to involve the most transparent decision-making procedures. While supranational and inter-governmental decision-making are the least transparent modes of governance, involving secret deliberations and secret negotiations respectively, open co-ordination and other 'soft' modes of governance that are growing in importance in EU decision-making can be seen on the one hand to increase openness and on the other to complicate the picture in terms of transparency.

Overall, the greatest problems before the Union today in terms of political responsibility from the point of view of the institutional structure concern the development of the forum side of accountability and, in many respects, identifiability. Both are closely associated with the Union's great diversity and the complex arrangements that have been put together to accommodate that very diversity. These are the challenges to responsible governance but also the building blocks from which political co-operation and a new moral community are slowly and gradually being built.

From the Constitutional Treaty to the Lisbon Treaty

At the moment of writing, it seems that the failure to approve the Constitutional Treaty is final. In the aftermath of the negative results of referenda that were meant to approve the Constitutional Treaty in France and the Netherlands in 2005, the Union was led to a long period of reflection, during which it became clear that a significant minority of member states, including the United Kingdom and Denmark, might also reject the Treaty in a referendum. Finally, after the election of Nicolas Sarkozy as French president and just before Tony Blair stepped down British prime minister, the German chancellor Angela Merkel undertook an initiative to revive the issue in June 2007. Her argument was that the Union of 27 would not be able to function without a new Treaty endorsing the major institutional innovations introduced by the Constitutional Treaty, and the aim should be to get this out of the way before the 2009 European elections.

In the June 2007 IGC the Lisbon Treaty was drafted, which kept most of the provisions of the Constitutional Treaty but did away with all references to a Constitution and the more symbolic elements, such as the Union flag, anthem and other symbols. It relinquished those elements of the Constitutional Treaty that might provoke negative reactions from those whose concern was the loss of national sovereignty: the name of the Treaty itself, the merging of previous Treaties into one, and the title of Foreign Minister of the Union. The European Charter of Fundamental Rights was annexed to the Lisbon Treaty, where it made up the second part of the Constitutional Treaty. Those institutional reforms that reflected an increased role of the member states, such as the role of national parliaments and the long-term European Council Presidency, were maintained and even reinforced. The question of QMV was yet again opened by the Poles during the IGC, and concessions had to be made. The new double majority system (fifty-five per cent of states and sixty-five per cent of the population with a blocking minority of four states) introduced with the Constitutional Treaty, which is designed to do away with the complicated weighed voting system, will be applied, but only as from 2014 instead of as from 2009. Opt-outs to parts of the Treaty were also negotiated by the United Kingdom and others. Finally, the form of the Treaty changed as well: since it did not incorporate the Treaty of the European Community or any other Treaties, it was presented as a series of amendments to previous Treaties, resulting in greater complexity and detail. The October 2007 IGC approved the Lisbon Treaty, which is set to be ratified by national parliaments and not by referenda across the twenty-seven member states, with the exception of the Republic of Ireland, where a crucial referendum is imminent.

The answer to whether the Constitutional and Lisbon Treaties represent an advance or a step backwards for the EU's responsibility deficit is rather mixed. In some cases, significant steps in the direction of remedying the responsibility deficit were made with the Constitutional Treaty, and these are being maintained or even reinforced with the Lisbon Treaty. The Council's increased openness when it acts in legislative mode was formalised in the Constitutional Treaty and has made it to the Lisbon Treaty. The new role of national parliaments in safeguarding subsidiarity, thus constituting an extra accountability check on the initiatives of the European Commission, has not only been reiterated but slightly strengthened in the Lisbon Treaty. Moving to QMV as a default procedure with exceptions in very few policy areas represents a major step in simplification and clarity in the Union's law-making, which is a positive point for identifiability.

In other cases, the Constitutional Treaty introduced new problems for responsibility, which the Lisbon Treaty reiterated. The most typical, explored in Chapter 4, has to do with the further complication of the executive. The Constitutional Treaty creates, and the Lisbon Treaty maintains, a problem of many heads for the Union, involving the addition of the offices of the double-hatted High Representative based in both Commission and Council and the long-term European Council president to the list of EU leaders, which includes the president of the Commission. The Council presidency system is further complicated as it will be run by a troika in rotation, while the presidencies of Council formations will no longer coincide with the presidency of the European Council. All of this is to the detriment of identifiability and possibly the check side of accountability.

In addition, some aspects of the Lisbon Treaty represent a retrenchment from the Constitutional Treaty from the point of view of responsibility. These mainly concern identifiability, which, along with the forum side of accountability, was argued to represent the principal shortcoming in the EU in terms of the institutional side of political responsibility. Two examples will be given here, both involving identifiability. The lesser concerns the fact that the implementation of the simpler QMV system without weighed voting in the Council has been postponed until 2014. The graver one has to do with the change in the form of the text that the Lisbon Treaty represents with respect to the Constitutional Treaty. One of the four main aims of the Laeken Declaration, which set out the mandate for the Convention on the Future of Europe, was the simplification of the Treaties in response to the need for citizens to gain an understanding of how the Union works. The Constitutional Treaty was an exercise in simplification with respect to the merging of the Treaties, the legislative procedures, legal instruments, competences and the form of the text itself. It resembled more a Constitution than a Treaty, at least with regard to Parts 1 and 2. This has by and large been undone with the new form given to the Lisbon Treaty.

European Governance, Monnet and the virtues of responsibility

The responsibility deficit that has been documented has serious implications for the EU. It was argued in Chapter 2 that when the practice of accountability and the presence of identifiability and openness in EU institutions work in combination, they can be expected to foster the development of the virtues of political responsibility in the context of the practice of governance. Clearly the gaps in their operation fail to encourage the flourishing of such virtues among all the participants to the practice of EU governance: politicians, officials, groups and citizens. They also contribute to a significant set of goods internal to the practice of EU governance not being fully achieved. The reference here is to order, stability and predictability.

From the point of view of responsible governance (the conception of which was set out in previous chapters), this state of affairs is at the core of the problem of legitimacy of EU governance. Not only is it problematic for the legitimacy of a practice when the virtues are not exercised and the goods internal to practices not sufficiently achieved, but also, from the point of view of the communitarian account of legitimacy, the weakness of subpractices of internal scrutiny – such as accountability is to governance – means that the very possibility of evaluating the legitimacy of the practice is weak, in the sense that it becomes less clear which canons we are to use.

So far, the glass has been seen to be half-empty, but it could as easily be taken to be half-full. For one, the lack of the virtues and the partial failure to achieve goods is not just due to the institutions and the extent to which they support accountability, identifiability and openness. It is also due to the more general weakness of moral community in the Union. The building up of a community through the uploading and downloading of practices and virtues until there is loose convergence around one conception of the good may also be expected to involve the exchange, circulation and establishment of the best practices of accountability, of which the Union, its nations and communities have much to boast of and draw from. It could well be argued that the practices of accountability established at EU level at present are themselves the result of such a process.

Furthermore, what was demonstrated in Chapters 3, 4 and 5 is that the trend with respect to the practice of accountability and its institutional supports – identifiability and openness – has generally been one of improvement in recent years, particularly after the 1999 crisis. The Santer Commission's resignation crisis was certainly one of the principal episodes that led to changes in this direction. Does this mean that the Monnet conception of responsibility in the practice of European governance is becoming less prominent?

The Monnet conception involved a one-sided emphasis on the virtues of responsibility by a technocratic elite and a disregard for the institutional conditions of responsibility. Its drawbacks, discussed extensively in Chapter 1, by and large contributed to the lack of the virtues of responsibility in the European Commission, which became evident in the Santer Commission resignation crisis. What has clearly begun to change in the post-Maastricht debate is the greater emphasis and concern with regard to the institutional side of political responsibility (Tsakatika 2005). Accountability, identifiability and openness were highlighted as problems and reforms were made. As for the virtues of political responsibility, they can be expected to take their time to flourish in the moral community that the EU is developing into. Until that happens we can be confident that the institutions are now slightly better equipped to encourage responsible men and women to play their part in governance.

References

Abbott, D. (2002) 'The Media's Contribution to Transparency', in V. Deckmyn (ed.) *Increasing Transparency in the European Union?* (Maastricht: EIPA).

Adkins, A. W. H. (1960) *Merit and Responsibility: A Study in Greek Values* (Oxford: Clarendon Press).

Adler, E. (2005) *Communitarian International Relations. The Epistemic Foundations of International Relations* (London and New York: Routledge).

Aristotle (1976) *The Nicomachean Ethics*. Translated by J. A. K. Thomson; Introduction and Bibliography by Jonathan Barnes (Harmondsworth: Penguin).

Armstrong, K., and Bulmer, S. (1997) *The Governance of the Single European Market* (Manchester: Manchester University Press).

Arnull, A. (2002) 'Introduction: The European Union's Accountability and Legitimacy Deficit', in A. Arnull and D. Wincott (eds) *Accountability and Legitimacy in the European Union* (Oxford: Oxford University Press).

Aspinwall, M. D., and Schneider, G. (2000) 'Same Menu, Separate Tables: The Institutionalist Turn in Political Science and the Study of European Integration', *European Journal of Political Research*, 38: 1–36.

Attucci, C., and Bellamy, R. (2007) 'Between Contract and Community: Normative Theory and the European Union', Paper presented at the UACES Workshop 'Values and the EU', June 2007, Edinburgh.

Auel, K. (2007) 'Democratic Accountability and National Parliaments: Redefining the Impact of Parliamentary Scrutiny in EU Affairs', *European Law Journal*, 13(4): 487–504.

—— (2005) 'Introduction: The Europeanisation of Parliamentary Democracy', *The Journal of Legislative Studies*, 11(3/4): 303–18.

Azzi, G. C. (1999) 'Comitology and the European Commission', in C. Joerges and E. Vos (eds) *EU Committees: Social Regulation, Law and Politics* (Oxford: Hart).

Banchoff, T., and Smith, M. P. (1999) *Legitimacy and the European Union: The Contested Polity* (London: Routledge).

Barker, A. (1998) 'Political Responsibility for UK Prison Security – Ministers Escape Again', *Public Administration*, 76(2): 1–23.

Bauer, M. (2004) 'Transparency in the Council', in M. Westlake and D. Galloway (2004) *The Council of the European Union*, 3rd edn (London: John Harper).

Beaud, O. (2000) 'Le principe de responsabilité politique à la concurrence d'autres formes de responsabilité des gouvernantes', *Pouvoirs*, 92: 17–30.

Beetham, D., and Lord, C. (1998) *Legitimacy and the European Union* (London: Longman).

Bellamy, R., and Castiglione, D. (2003) 'Legitimizing the Euro-"Polity" and its "Regime": The Normative Turn in EU Studies', *European Journal of Political Theory*, 2(1): 7–34.

—— (2000) 'Democracy, Sovereignty and the Construction of the European Union: The Republican Alternative to Liberalism', in Z. Bankowski and A. Scott (eds) *The European Union and its Order* (London: Blackwell).

—— (1997) 'Building the Union: The Nature of Sovereignty in the Political Architecture of Europe', *Law and Philosophy*, 16(4): 421–45.

Bellamy, R., and Warleigh, A. (eds) (2001) *Citizenship and Governance in the European Union* (London: Continuum).

Bentham, J. (1962) 'An Essay on Political Tactics', in *The Works of Jeremy Bentham*, vol. 7, 299–373 (New York: Russel and Russel Inc).

Bergman, T. (2000) 'Introduction: Delegation and Accountability in European Integration', in T. Bergman and E. Damgaard (eds) *Delegation and Accountability in European Integration: The Nordic Parliamentary Democracies and the European Union* (London: Frank Cass).

Birch, A. H. (1964) *Representative and Responsible Government: An Essay on the British Constitution* (London: Allen and Unwin).

Bjurulf, B., and Elgström, O. (2004) 'Negotiating Transparency: The Role of Institutions', *Journal of Common Market Studies*, 42(2): 249–69.

Blair, T. (2000) Speech to the Polish Stock Exchange, Warsaw, 6 October.

Blavoukos, S., Bourantonis, D., and Pagoulatos, G. (2007) 'A President for the European Union: A New Actor in Town?', *Journal of Common Market Studies*, 45(2): 231–52.

Blum, L. (1996) 'Community and Virtue', in R. Crisp (ed.) *How Should One Live? Essays on the Virtues* (Oxford: Clarendon Press).

Bok, S. (1984) *Secrets: On the Ethics of Concealment and Revelation* (Oxford: Oxford University Press).

Borrás, S., and Jacobsson, K. (2004) 'The Open Method of Co-ordination and New Governance Patterns in the EU', *Journal of European Public Policy*, 11(2): 185–208.

Börzel, T., and Sprungk, C. (2007) 'Undermining Democratic Governance in the Member States? The Europeanization of National Decision-Making', in Ronald Holzhacker and Erik Albaek (eds) *Democratic Governance and European Integration* (Cheltenham: Edward Elgar).

Börzel, T. A., and Risse, T. (2000) 'Who is Afraid of a European Federation? How to Constitutionalize a Multi-Level Governance System', in C. Joerges, Y. Mény and J. H. H. Weiler (eds) *What Kind of Constitution for What Kind of Polity? Responses to Joschka Fischer* (Florence: European University Institute).

Bovens, M. (1998) *The Quest for Responsibility: Accountability and Citizenship in Complex Organisations* (Cambridge: Cambridge University Press).

Bradley, K. (1999) 'Institutional Aspects of Comitology: Scenes from the Cutting Room Floor', in C. Joerges and E. Vos (eds) *EU Committees: Social Regulation, Law and Politics* (Oxford: Hart).

Brennan, G., and Pettit, P. (1990) 'Unveiling the Vote', *British Journal of Political Science*, 20(3): 311–33.

Büchs, M. (2008) 'The Open Method of Coordination as a "Two-Level Game"', *Policy and Politics*, 36 (1): 21-37.

Bulmer, S. (1997) 'New Institutionalism, the Single Market and EU Governance',

ARENA Working Papers, WP 97/25.

de Búrca, G., and de Witte, B. (2002) 'The Delimitation of Powers Between the EU and its Member States', in A. Arnull and D. Wincott (eds) *Accountability and Legitimacy in the European Union* (Oxford: Oxford University Press).

Burgess, M. (1991) *Federalism and European Union: Political Ideas, Influences and Strategies in the European Community, 1972–1987* (London: Routledge).

—— (1986) 'Altiero Spinelli, Federalism and the EUT', in J. Lodge (ed.) *European Union: the European Community in Search of a Future* (London: Macmillan).

Burley, A. M., and Mattli, W. (1993) 'Europe Before the Court: A Political Theory of Integration', *International Organisation*, 47(1): 41–76.

Cameron, F., and Spence, D. (2004) 'The Commission–Council Tandem in the Foreign Policy Arena', in D. G. Dimitrakopoulos (ed.) *The Changing European Commission* (Manchester: Manchester University Press).

Checkel, J. (1998) 'The Constructivist Turn in International Relations Theory', *World Politics*, 50(2): 324–48.

Chiatelli, C. (2006) 'The Reform of the Lisbon Strategy's Governance Framework – Is "New Governance" the Way Forward?', *Journal of Contemporary European Research*, 2(1): 4–20.

Christiansen, T., Joergensen, K. E., and Wiener, A. (eds) (2001) *The Social Construction of Europe* (London: Sage).

—— (1999) 'The Social Construction of Europe', *Journal of European Public Policy*, 6(4): 528–44.

Christiansen, T., and Kirchner, E. (2000) 'Introduction', in T. Christiansen and E. Kirchner (eds) *Committee Governance in the European Union* (Manchester: Manchester University Press).

Chryssochoou, D. (2002) 'Europe's Republican Moment', *Journal of European Integration*, 24(4): 341–57.

Commission of the European Communities, Transparency web site http://ec.europa. eu/transparency/index_en.htm.

Commission of the European Communities (2007) Green Paper. *Public Access to Documents Held by Institutions of the European Community. A Review*. COM (2007), 185 final. Brussels, 18 April 2007.

—— (2006) Green Paper. *European Transparency Initiative*. COM (2006), 194 final. Brussels, 3 May 2006.

—— (2001) *European Governance: A White Paper*. COM (2001), 428 final. Brussels, 25 July 2001.

—— (1993) *Public Access to the Institutions' Documents. Interinstitutional Declaration on Democracy, Transparency and Subsidiarity*. COM (1993) 191, Brussels, 5 May 1993.

Convention on the Future of Europe (2002) *Final Report of Working Group IX on Simplification* (CONV 424/02).

COSAC web site www.cosac.eu/en/.

Costa, P. (2004) 'From National to European Citizenship: A Historical Comparison', in R. Bellamy, D. Castiglione and E. Santoro (eds) *Lineages of European Citizenship. Rights, Belonging and Participation in Eleven Nation-States* (Basingstoke: Palgrave Macmillan).

Council of the European Union (2000a) 'Decision of the Secretary General of the Council/High Representative for the Common Foreign and Security Policy on Measures for the Protection of Classified Information Applicable to the General Secretariat of the Council', *Official Journal of the European Communities*,

2000/C 239/01, 27 July 2000.

Council of the European Union. General Secretariat (2000b) *The Council's Rules of Procedure* (Luxembourg: Office for Official Publications of the European Communities).

—— (1993) *The Council's Rules of Procedure* (Luxembourg: Office for Official Publications of the European Communities).

Craig, P. (2004) 'The Constitutional Treaty: Legislative and Executive Power in the Emerging Constitutional Order', *EUI Working Paper* LAW, no. 2004/7.

Crum, B. (2003) 'Legislative-Executive Relations in the European Union', *Journal of Common Market Studies*, 41(3): 375–95.

Curtin, D. (2007) 'Holding (Quasi-) Autonomous EU Administrative Actors to Public Account', *European Law Journal*, 13(4): 523–41.

Dagger, R. (1997) *Civic Virtues: Rights, Citizenship and Republican Liberalism* (Oxford: Oxford University Press).

Dehousse, R. (1999) 'Towards a Regulation of Transnational Governance? Citizens' Rights and the Reform of Comitology Procedures', in C. Joerges and E. Vos (eds) *EU Committees: Social Regulation, Law and Politics* (Oxford: Hart).

Dobson, L. (2006) *Supranational Citizenship* (Manchester: Manchester University Press).

Dobson, L., and Føllesdal, A. (eds) (2004) *Political Theory and the European Constitution* (London: Routledge).

Docksey, C., and Williams, K. (1997) 'The European Commission and the Execution of Community Policy', in G. Edwards and D. Spence (eds) *The European Commission* (Harlow: Longman).

Dowding, K. (2000) 'Institutional Research on the European Union; A Critical Review', *European Union Politics*, 1(1): 125–44.

Duchacek, I. D. (1973) *Power Map: Comparative Politics of Constitutions* (Oxford: ABC Clio).

Duchêne, F. (1996) 'Jean Monnet – Pragmatic Visionary', in M. Bond, J. Smith and W. Wallace (eds) *Eminent Europeans: Personalities who Shaped Contemporary Europe* (London: The Greycoat Press).

Duggett, M. (2000) 'Jean Monnet and Project Management: Some Reflections on Originality in Public Administration', *Public Policy and Administration*, 15(1), 77–83.

Duina, F., and Raunio, T. (2007) 'The Open Method of Co-ordination and National Parliaments: Further Marginalization or New Opportunities?' *Journal of European Public Policy*, 14(4): 489–506.

Dunn, J. (1990) *Interpreting Political Responsibility* (Cornwall: Polity Press).

Dyrberg, P. (2002) 'Accountability and Legitimacy: What is the Contribution of Transparency?', in A. Arnull and D. Wincott (eds) *Accountability and Legitimacy in the European Union* (Oxford: Oxford University Press).

Dyson, K., and Featherstone, K. (1996) 'Italy and EMU as "Vincolo Esterno": Empowering the Technocrats, Transforming the State', *South European Society and Politics*, 1(2): 272–99.

Editorial Comments (1999) 'The Report of the Committee of Independent Experts: An Ill Wind…', *Common Market Law Review*, 36(2): 269–72.

van der Eijk, C., and Franklin, M. N. (2004) 'Potential for Contestation on European Matters at National Elections in Europe', in G. Marks and M. R. Steenbergen (eds) *European Integration and Political Conflict* (Cambridge: Cambridge University Press).

Eising, R., and Kohler-Koch, B. (1999) 'Governance in the European Union: A Comparative Assessment', in B. Kohler-Koch and R. Eising (eds) *The Transformation of Governance in the European Union* (London: Routledge).

Eriksen, E. O., and Fossum, J. E. (eds) (2000) *Democracy in the European Union – Integration through Deliberation?* (London: Routledge).

Etzioni, A. (2007) 'The Community Deficit', *Journal of Common Market Studies*, 45(1): 23–42.

European Ombudsman (1998) 'Special Report from the European Ombudsman to the European Parliament Following the Own-Initiative Inquiry into Public Access to Documents' (616/PUBAC/F/IJH), *Official Journal of the European Communities*, C44/9-13, 10 February 1998.

European Parliament and Council (2001) 'Regulation of the European Parliament and Council Regarding Public Access to European Parliament, Council and Commission Documents 2001 on Transparency' no. 1049/2001. *Official Journal of the European Communities*, L145/43, 30 May 2001.

Fearon, J. D. (1999) 'Electoral Accountability and the Control of Politicians: Selecting Good Types versus Sanctioning Poor Performance', in B. Manin, A. Przeworski and S. C. Stokes (eds) *Democracy, Accountability and Representation* (Cambridge: Cambridge University Press).

Featherstone, K. (1994) 'Jean Monnet and the "Democratic Deficit" in the European Union', *Journal of Common Market Studies*, 32 (2): 149–70.

Feinberg, J. (1970) *Doing and Deserving: Essays in the Theory of Responsibility* (New Jersey: Princeton University Press).

First Report on Allegation Regarding Fraud, Mismanagement and Nepotism in the European Commission (1999), available at http://www.europarl.europa.eu/experts/report1_en.htm. Accessed 7 May 2008.

Fischer, J. (2000) 'From Confederacy to Federation: Thoughts on the Finality of European Integration'. Speech by Joschka Fischer at the Humboltd University in Berlin, 12 May, available at www.auswaertiges-amt.de/www/en/infoservice.

Fischer, J. M., and Ravizza, M. (1998) *Responsibility and Control: A Theory of Moral Responsibility* (Cambridge: Cambridge University Press).

Føllesdal, A. (2006) 'Survey Article: The Legitimacy Deficits of the European Union', *Journal of Political Philosophy*, 14(4): 441–68.

—— (1998) 'Democracy, Legitimacy and Majority Rule in the EU', in A. Weale and M. Nentwich (eds) *Political Theory and the European Union: Legitimacy, Constitutional Choice and Citizenship* (London: Routledge).

—— and Hix, S. (2006) 'Why There Is a Democratic Deficit in the EU: A Response to Majone and Moravcsik', *Journal of Common Market Studies*, 44(3): 533–62.

—— and Koslowski, R. (eds) (1998) *Democracy and the European Union* (Berlin: Springer).

Frazer, E., and Lacey, N. (1994) 'MacIntyre, Feminism and the Concept of Practice', in J. Horton and S. Mendus (eds) *After MacIntyre: Critical Perspectives on the Work of Alasdair MacIntyre* (Notre Dame: University of Notre Dame Press).

Garrett, G. (1995) 'The Politics of Legal Integration in the European Union', *International Organization*, 49(1): 171–81.

—— (1992) 'International Co-operation and Institutional Choice: The European Community's Internal Market', *International Organization*, 46(2): 533–60.

——, Keleman R. D., and Schultz, H. (1998) 'The European Court of Justice, National Governments and Legal Integration in the European Union', *International Organization*, 52(1): 149–76.

Gillingham, J. (1991) 'Jean Monnet and the European Coal and Steel Community: A Preliminary Appraisal', in D. Brinkley and C. Hackett (eds) *Jean Monnet: The Path to European Unity* (London: Macmillan).

Goodin, R. (1992) *Motivating Political Morality* (Cambridge, Mass.: Blackwell).

Goldman, A. I. (1999) 'Why Citizens Should Vote: A Causal Responsibility Approach', *Social Philosophy and Policy*, 16(2): 201–17.

Gregory, R. (1998) 'Political Responsibility for Bureaucratic Incompetence: Tragedy at Cave Creek', *Public Administration*, 76: 519–38.

Grey, P. (1998) 'Policy Disasters in Europe: An Introduction', in P. Grey and P. t'Hart (eds) *Public Policy Disasters in Western Europe* (London: Routledge).

Grimm, D. (1995) 'Does Europe need a Constitution?', *European Law Journal*, 1(3): 282–302.

Haas, E. B. (1958) *The Uniting of Europe: Political, Social and Economic Forces, 1950–1957* (Stanford: Stanford University Press).

Habermas, J. (2001) 'Why Europe Needs a Constitution', *New Left Review*, 11: 5–26.

—— (1996) *Between Facts and Norms* (Cambridge: Polity Press).

—— (1995) 'Remarks to Peter Grimm's: Does Europe Need a Constitution?', *European Law Journal*, 1(3): 303–7.

Hall, P. A., and Taylor, R. C. R. (1996) 'Political Science and the Three New Institutionalisms', *Political Studies*, 44, 936–57.

Hamilton, A., Madison, J., and Jay, J. [1788] (2000) *The Federalist, or, The New Constitution* (London: Phoenix).

Harlow, C. (2002) *Accountability in the European Union* (Oxford: Oxford University Press).

Hart, H. L. A. (1968) *Punishment and Responsibility* (Oxford: Oxford University Press).

Herrmann, R. K., Risse, T., and Brewer, M. B. (eds) (2004) *Transnational Identities: Becoming European in the EU* (Oxford: Rowman and Littlefield).

Haydon, G. (1978) 'On Being Responsible', *Philosophical Quarterly*, 28: 46–57.

Hayward, J. (1996) 'Conclusion: Has European Unification by Stealth a Future?', in J. Hayward (ed.) *Elitism, Populism, and European Politics* (Oxford: Clarendon Press).

Heyes-Renshaw, F. (2006) 'The Council of Ministers', in J. Peterson and M. Shackleton (eds) *The Institutions of the European Union* (Oxford: Oxford University Press).

—— and Wallace, H. (1997) *The Council of Ministers* (London: Macmillan).

Hix, S. (2005) *The Political System of the European Union*, 2nd edn (London: Palgrave Macmillan).

——, Kreppel, A., and Noury, A. (2003) 'The Party System in the European Parliament: Collusive or Competitive?', *Journal of Common Market Studies*, 41(2): 309–31.

—— and Lord, C (1996) 'The Making of a President: The European Parliament and the Confirmation of Jacques Santer as President of the Commission', *Government and Opposition*, 62–76.

Hobbes [1651] (1985) *Leviathan*, edited with an introduction by C. B. Macpherson (Harmondsworth: Penguin).

Hodson, D., and Maher, I. (2001) 'The Open Method as a New Mode of Governance: The Case of Soft Law Economic Policy Co-ordination', *Journal of Common Market Studies*, 39(4): 719–45.

Hollis, M. (1994) *The Philosophy of Social Science: An Introduction* (Cambridge: Cambridge University Press).

Hoskyns, C., and Newman, M. (eds) (2000) *Democratizing the European Union* (Manchester: Manchester University Press).

Hüller, T. (2007) 'Assessing EU Strategies for Publicity', *Journal of European Public Policy*, 14(4): 563–81.

Hume, D. [1742] (1889) 'Of the Independency of Parliament', in *Essays Literary, Moral and Political*, edited by T. H. Green and T. H. Grose (London: Longmans, Green and Co.).

Jimenez, F. (1998) 'Political Scandals and Political Responsibility in Democratic Spain', *West European Politics*, 21(4): 80–99.

Joerges, C. (1999) '"Good Governance" through Comitology?', in C. Joerges and E. Vos (eds) *EU Committees: Social Regulation, Law and Politics* (Oxford: Hart).

—— (2002) 'Deliberative Supranationalism: Two Defences', *European Law Journal*, 8(1): 133–51.

—— and Neyer, J. (1997) 'From Intergovernmental Bargaining to Deliberative Political Processes: The Constitutionalization of Comitology', *European Law Journal*, 3(3): 273–99.

Judge, D., and Earnshaw, D. (2003) *The European Parliament* (Houndmills: Palgrave Macmillan).

Jupile, J., and Caporaso, J. A. (1999) 'Institutionalism in the European Union: Beyond International Relations and Comparative Politics', *Annual Review of Political Science*, 2: 429–44.

Kallas, S. (2006) 'Transparency Restores Confidence in Europe', Speech at the European Policy Institutes Network, Centre of European Policy Studies, Brussels, 20 October 2005.

Kay, R. (1998) 'American Constitutionalism', in L. Alexander (ed.) *Constitutionalism: Philosophical Foundations* (Cambridge: Cambridge University Press).

Kertzer, D. I. (1988) *Ritual, Politics and Power* (New Haven and London: Yale University Press).

Kiewet, D. R., and McCubbins, M. D. (1991) *The Logic of Delegation: Congressional Parties and the Appropriations Process* (Chicago: The University of Chicago Press).

Kohler-Koch, B., and Rittberger, B. (2006) 'Review Article: The Governance Turn in EU Studies', *Journal of Common Market Studies*, 44(1): 27–49.

Kohnstamm, M. (1990) 'Jean Monnet and the European Community in the 1990's', *Irish Studies in International Affairs*, 3(2): 5–13.

Kreppel, A. (1999) 'The European Parliament's Influence over EU Policy Outcomes', *Journal of Common Market Studies*, 37(3): 521–38.

Laeken Declaration (2001) Presidency Conclusions, Annex 1. Laeken, 14–15 December, 2001. http://europa.eu/bulletin/en/200112/i1027.htm.

Laffan, B., and Shaw, C. (2005) 'Classifying and Mapping OMC in Different Policy Areas'. Report for NEWGOV New Modes of Governance (Integrated Project Priority 7: Citizens and Governance in the Knowledge-based Society). http:// eucenter.wisc.edu/OMC/Papers/laffanShaw.pdf.

Larsson, T. (1998) 'How Open Can a Government be?', in V. Deckmyn and I. Thomson (eds) *Openness and Transparency in the European Union* (Maastricht: EIPA).

Lehning, P. (1997) 'Pluralism, Contractarianism and Europe', in P. Lehning and

A. Weale (eds) *Citizenship, Democracy and Justice in the New Europe* (London: Routledge).

Lindberg, L. N. (1963) *The Political Dynamics of European Economic Integration* (Stanford: Stanford University Press).

Linklater, A. (1998) *The Transformation of Political Community: Ethical Foundations of the Post-Westphalian Era* (Cambridge: Polity Press).

Lodge, J. (1994) 'Transparency and Democratic Legitimacy', *Journal of Common Market Studies*, 32(3): 343–68.

Lord, C. (1998) *Democracy in the European Union* (Sheffield: Sheffield Academic Press).

Lord, C., and Harris, E. (2006) *Democracy in the New Europe* (Houndmills: Palgrave Macmillan).

Lucas, J. R. (1993) *Responsibility* (Oxford: Clarendon Press).

Lupia, A. (2000) 'The EU, the EEA and Domestic Accountability: How Outside Forces Affect Delegation within Member-States', in T. Bergman and E. Damgaard (eds) *Delegation and Accountability in European Integration: The Nordic Parliamentary Democracies and the European Union* (London: Frank Cass).

Lutz, C. S. (2004) *Tradition in the Ethics of Alasdair MacIntyre: Relativism, Thomism and Philosophy* (Oxford: Lexington).

MacCormick, N. (1997) 'Democracy, Subsidiarity and Citizenship in the "European Commonwealth"', *Law and Philosophy*, 16: 331–56.

MacIntyre, A. (1998) 'Politics Philosophy and the Common Good', in K. Knight (ed.) *The MacIntyre Reader* (Notre Dame: University of Notre Dame Press).

—— (1994) 'A Partial Response to my Critics', in J. Horton and S. Mendus (eds) *After MacIntyre. Critical Perspectives on the Work of Alasdair MacIntyre* (Notre Dame: University of Notre Dame Press).

—— (1989) *Dependent Rational Animals: Why Human Beings Need the Virtues* (Chicago: Open Court).

—— (1988) *Whose Justice? Which Rationality?* (Notre Dame: University of Notre Dame Press).

—— (1984) 'Is Patriotism a Virtue?' Lindley Lecture at the University of Kansas. Cited to reprinted version in R. Beiner (ed.) (1995) *Theorizing Citizenship* (New York: State University of New York Press).

—— (1981) *After Virtue: A Study in Moral Theory* (London: Duckworth).

MacMullen, A. (2000) 'European Commissioners: National Routes to a European Elite', in N. Nugent (ed.) *At the Heart of the Union: Studies of the European Commission* 2nd edn (London: Macmillan).

—— (1999) 'Political Responsibility for the Administration of Europe: The Commission's Resignation March 1999', *Parliamentary Affairs*, 52(4), 703–18.

McNamara, K. R. (2006) 'Managing the Euro: the European Central Bank', in J. Peterson and M. Shackleton (eds) *The Institutions of the European Union*, 2nd edn (Oxford: Oxford University Press).

Magnette, P. (2006) 'Democracy in the European Union: Why and How to Combine Representation and Participation?', in S. Smismans (ed.) *Civil Society and Legitimate European Governance* (Cheltenham: Edward Elgar).

—— (2004) 'Deliberation or Bargaining? Coping with Constitutional Conflicts in the Convention on the Future of Europe', in E. O. Eriksen, J. E. Fossum and A. J. Menendez (eds) (2004) *Developing a Constitution for Europe* (London:

Routledge).

—— (2003) *What Is the European Union: Nature and Prospects* (London: Palgrave Macmillan).

Majone, G. (1996a) 'Theories of Regulation', in G. Majone (1996) *Regulating Europe* (London and New York: Routledge).

—— (1996b) 'Regulatory Legitimacy', in G. Majone (1996) *Regulating Europe* (London and New York: Routledge).

—— (1994) 'Independence vs Accountability? Non-Majoritarian Institutions and Democratic Government in Europe', *EUI Working Papers*, 94/3 (Florence: EUI).

—— (1993) 'The European Community: An Independent Fourth Branch of Government?' *EUI Working Papers*, 93/9 (Florence: EUI).

Mamadouh, V., and Raunio, T. (2003) 'The Committee System: Powers, Appointments and Report Allocation', *Journal of Common Market Studies*, 41(2): 333–51.

Manin, B., Przeworski, A., and Stokes, C. S. (1999) 'Elections and Representation', in B. Manin, A. Przeworski and C. S. Stokes (eds) *Democracy, Accountability and Representation* (Cambridge: Cambridge University Press).

March, J. G., and Olsen, J. P. (1984) 'The New Institutionalism: Organisational Factors in Political Life', *American Political Science Review*, 78: 734–49.

—— (1995) *Democratic Governance* (New York: The Free Press).

Markovits, A. S., and Silverstein, M. (1988) 'Introduction: Power and Process in Liberal Democracies', in A. S. Markovits and M. Silverstein (eds) *The Politics of Scandal: Power and Process in Liberal Democracies* (New York and London: Holmes and Maier).

Marks, G. (1997) 'A Third Lens: Comparing European Integration and State Building', in J. Klausen and L. A. Tilly (eds) *European Integration in Social and Historical Perspective* (Oxford : Rowman and Littlefield).

Marks, G., Hooghe, L., and Blank, K. (1996) 'European Integration from the 1980s: State-Centric vs Multi-Level Governance', *Journal of Common Market Studies*, 34(3): 341–78.

Mason, A. (2000) *Community, Solidarity and Belonging: Levels of Community and their Normative Significance* (Cambridge: Cambridge University Press).

—— (1996) 'MacIntyre on Modernity and How It Has Marginalised the Virtues', in R. Crisp (ed.) *How Should One Live?* (Oxford: Oxford University Press).

Maurer, A., and Wessels, W. (eds) (2001) *National Parliaments on their Ways to Europe: Losers or Latecomers?* (Nomos: Baden Baden).

Mayer, F. (2004) 'Competences-Reloaded? The Vertical Division of Power in the EU After the New European Constitution', in J. H. H. Weiler and C. L. Eisgruber (eds) *Altneuland: The EU Constitution in a Contextual Perspective*, Jean Monnet Working Paper 5/04, www.jeanmonnetprogram.org/papers/04/040501-16.html.

Micklitz, H. W., and Weatherhill, S. (1994) 'Federalism and Responsibility', in H. W. Micklitz, T. Roethe and S. Weatherhill (eds) *Federalism and Responsibility: A Study on Product Safety Law and Practice in the European Community* (London: Graham and Trotman).

Mill, J. S. [1861](1991) *On Liberty and Other Essays*, edited with an introduction by J. Gray (Oxford: Oxford University Press).

Minz, D. H. (2006) Draft Report on the Special Report from the European Ombudsman following the draft recommendation to the Council of the

European Union in complaint 2395/2003/GG concerning the openness of the meetings of the Council when acting in its legislative capacity. Committee on Petitions, PE 367.904v01-00, 18 January 2006.

Monnet, J. (1978) *Memoirs* (London: Collins).

Moravcsik, A. (2002) 'In Defence of the "democratic deficit": Reassessing Legitimacy in the European Union, *Journal of Common Market Studies*, 40(4): 603–24.

—— (1998) *The Choice for Europe: Social Purpose and State Power from Messina to Maastricht* (Ithaca: Cornell University Press).

—— (1995) 'Liberal Intergovernmentalism and Integration: A Rejoinder', *Journal of Common Market Studies*, 33(4): 611–28.

—— (1993) 'Preferences and Power in the European Community: A Liberal Intergovernmentalist Approach' *Journal of Common Market Studies*, 31(4): 473–524.

—— (1991) 'Negotiating the Single European Act', in R. O. Keohane and S. Hoffman (eds) *The New European Community* (Boulder, Colorado: Westview Press).

Mulhall, S., and Swift, A. (1992) *Liberals and Communitarians* (Oxford: Blackwell).

Nagel, T. (1986) *The View from Nowhere* (Oxford: Oxford University Press).

Norman, P. (2003) *The Accidental Constitution: The Story of the European Convention* (Brussels: EuroComment).

Norton, P. (ed.) (1996) *National Parliaments and the European Union* (London: Frank Cass).

Nugent, N. (2001) *The European Commission* (Houndmills: Palgrave).

Page, E. C. (1997) *The Men Who Run Europe* (Oxford: Clarendon Press).

Papadopoulos, Y. (2007) 'Problems of Democratic Accountability in Network and Multilevel Governance' *European Law Journal*, 13(4): 469–86.

Pedler, R., and Bradley, K. (2006) 'The Commission, Policy Management and Comitology', in D. Spence and G. Edwards (eds) *The European Commission* (London: John Harper).

Pennock, J. R. (1979) *Democratic Political Theory* (Princeton, New Jersey: Princeton University Press).

Peters, B. G., and Pierre, J. (2004) 'Multi-level Governance and Democracy: A Faustian Bargain?', in I. Bache and M. Flinders (eds) *Multi-Level Governance* (Oxford: Oxford University Press).

Peterson, J. (1999) 'The Santer Era: the European Commission in Normative, Historical and Theoretical Perspective', *Journal of European Public Policy*, 6(1): 46–65.

—— (1997) 'The European Union: Pooled Sovereignty, Divided Accountability', *Political Studies*, 45: 559–78.

—— (1995) 'Decision-Making in the European Union: Towards a Framework for Analysis', *Journal of European Public Policy*, 2(1): 69–93.

Pettit, P. (1997) *Republicanism: A Theory of Freedom and Government* (Oxford: Clarendon Press).

Pierson, P. (1996) 'The Path to European Integration: A Historical Institutionalist Analysis', *Comparative Political Studies*, 29(2): 123–63.

Pisani-Ferry, J., and Sapir, A. (2006) 'Last Exit to Lisbon', *Bruegel Policy Brief*, Issue 2006/02, March 2006, www.bruegel.org/index.php?pid=73.

Pole, J. R. (1983) *The Gift of Government: Political Responsibility from the English Restoration to American Independence* (Athens: The University of Georgia Press).

Pollack, M. (2002) *The Engines of European Integration: Delegation, Agency and Agenda-Setting in the European Union* (Oxford: Oxford University Press).
—— (2001) 'International Relations Theory and European Integration', *Journal of Common Market Studies*, 39(2): 221–44.
—— (1997) 'Delegation, Agency and Agenda-Setting in the European Community', *International Organisation*, 51(1): 99–134.
—— (1996) 'The New Institutionalism and EC Governance: The Promise and Limits of Institutionalist Analysis', *Governance*, 9(4): 429–58.
—— (1995) 'Creeping Competencies: The Expanding Agenda of the European Community'. *Journal of Public Policy*, 29: 123–63.
Pollitt, C., and Bouckaert, G. (2000) *Public Management Reform: A Comparative Analysis* (Oxford: Oxford University Press).
Price, D. (1985) *America's Unwritten Constitution: Science, Religion and Political Responsibility* (Cambridge Mass.: Harvard University Press).
Raunio, T. (2005) 'Holding Governments Accountable in European Affairs: Explaining Cross-National Variation', *Journal of Legislative Studies*, 11(3–4): 319–42.
Rawls, J. (1993) *Political Liberalism* (New York: Columbia University Press).
Raz, J. (1994) *Ethics in the Public Domain: Essays in the Morality of Law and Politics* (Oxford: Clarendon Press).
Reform Treaty (2007) Draft Treaty Amending the Treaty on European Union and the Treaty Establishing the European Community, CIG/07, Brussels 23 July 2007.
Resolution on the Drafting of Community Legislation (1993) *Official Journal* 93/C 166/01, 8 June 1993.
Richardson, H. S. (1999) 'Institutionally Divided Moral Responsibility', *Social Philosophy and Policy*, Volume 16(2): 218–49.
Robertson, K. G. (1982) *Public Secrets: A Study in the Development of Governmental Secrecy* (London: Macmillan).
Rosamond, B. (2000) *Theories of European Integration* (London: Macmillan).
Rourke, F. E. (1961) *Secrecy and Publicity: Dilemmas of Democracy* (Baltimore: The Johns Hopkins Press).
Ruzza, C., and de la Sala, V. (eds) (2007) *Civil Society and Governance in the European Union, vol 1. Normative Perspectives* (Manchester: Manchester University Press).
Sabel, C., and Zeitlin, J. (2007) 'Learning from difference: the new architecture of the experimentalist governance of the European Union' *European Governance Papers (EUROGOV)*, no. C-07-02, www.connex-network.org/eurogov/pdf/egp-connex-C-07-02.pdf.
Sandholtz, W. (1993) 'Choosing Union: Monetary Politics and Maastricht', *International Organization*, 47(1): 1–40.
—— and Zysman, J. (1989) '1992: Recasting the European Bargain', *World Politics*, 41(1): 95–128.
Scanlon, T. M. (1988) 'The Significance of Choice', *The Tanner Lectures on Human Values*, v.8 (Salt Lake City: The University of Utah Press).
—— (1982) 'Contractualism and Utilitarianism', in A. Sen and B. Williams (eds) *Utilitarianism and Beyond* (Cambridge: Cambridge University Press).
Scharpf, F. (1997) *Games Real Actors Play: Actor-Centered Institutionalism in Policy Research* (Boulder: Westview).
—— (1988) 'The Joint Decision Trap: Lessons from German Federalism and

European Integration', *Public Administration*, 66: 239–78.

Schklar, J. (1990) *The Faces of Injustice* (New Haven and London: Yale University Press).

Schmitter, P. C. (1996) 'Examining the Present Euro-Polity with the Help of Past Theories', in G. Marks, F. Scharpf, P. Schmitter and W. Streek (eds) *Governance in the European Union* (London: Sage).

Scott, J., and Trubek, D. M. (2002) 'Mind the Gap: Law and New Approaches to Governance in the European Union', *European Law Journal* 8(1): 1–18.

Shapcott, R. (2001) *Justice, Community and Dialogue in International Relations* (Cambridge: Cambridge University Press).

Shaw, J. (2003) 'Process, Responsibility and Inclusion in the EU Constitutionalism', *European Law Journal*, 9(1): 45–68.

Searing, D. D. (1991) 'Roles, Rules and Rationality in the New Institutionalism', *American Political Science Review*, 85(4): 1239–58.

Smiley, M. (1992) *Moral Responsibility and the Boundaries of Community: Power and Accountability from a Pragmatic Point of View* (Chicago: The University of Chicago Press).

Smismans, S. (ed.) (2006) Civil *Society and Legitimate European Governance* (Cheltenham: Edward Elgar).

Smith, A. D. (1992) 'National Identity and the Idea of European Unity', *International Affairs*, 68(1): 55–76.

Strawson, P. F. (1968) 'Freedom and Resentment', in Strawson (ed.), *Studies in the Philosophy of Thought and Action* (Oxford: Oxford University Press).

Szyszczak, E. (2002) 'Social Policy in the Post-Nice Era', in A. Arnull and D. Wincott (eds) *Accountability and Legitimacy in the European Union* (Oxford: Oxford University Press).

Tant, T. (1988) 'Constitutional Aspects of Official Secrecy and Freedom of Information: An Overview', *Essex Papers in Politics and Government*, 52.

Thompson, D. (1980) 'Moral Responsibility of Public Officials: The Problem of Many Hands', *American Political Science Review*, 74, 905–16.

Treaty of Amsterdam Amending the Treaty on European Union, the Treaties Establishing the European Communities and Certain Related Acts (1997) (Luxembourg: Office for Official Publications of the European Communities).

Treaty Establishing the European Community (Consolidated Version). *Official Journal of the European Communities*, C340, 10 November 1997.

Treaty Establishing a Constitution for Europe. Official Journal of the European Communities, C310, 2004/C 310/01, volume 47, 16 December 2004.

Treaty on European Union (1992) (Luxembourg: Office for Official Publications of the European Communities).

Treaty of Nice. Amending the Treaty on European Union, the Treaties establishing the European Communities and certain related acts (2001) *Official Journal of the European Communities*, C80/1, 10 March 2001.

Tsakatika, M. (2007a) 'Governance vs Politics: The European Union's Constitutive Democratic "Deficit"', *Journal of European Public Policy*, 14(6): 867–85.

—— (2007b) 'A parliamentary dimension for EU soft governance', *Journal of European Integration*, 29(5): pp. 549-64.

—— (2005) 'Claims to Legitimacy: The European Commission between Continuity and Change', *Journal of Common Market Studies*, 43(1): 193–220.

—— (2004) 'The Open Method of Co-ordination in the European Convention: A Lost Opportunity'?, in A. Føllesdal and L. Dobson (eds) *Political Theory and the European Constitution* (London: Routledge).

Tsebelis, G. (1994) 'The Power of the European Parliament as Conditional Agenda-Setter', *American Political Science Review*, 88(1): 129–42.

—— and Garrett, G (1997) 'Agenda-Setting, Vetoes and the European Union's Co-decision Procedure', *Journal of Legislative Studies*, 3(3): 74–92.

Tully, J. (2007) 'A New Kind of Europe? Democratic Integration in the European Union', *Critical Review of International Social and Political Philosophy*, 10(1): 71–86.

Vile, M. J. C. (1967) *Constitutionalism and the Separation of Powers* (Oxford: Clarendon Press).

Vos, E. (1999) 'EU Committees: the Evolution of Unforeseen Institutional Actors in European Product Regulation', in C. Joerges and E. Vos (eds) *EU Committees: Social Regulation, Law and Politics* (Oxford: Hart).

Wagner, W. (2006) 'The Democratic Control of Military Power Europe', *Journal of European Public Policy*, 13(2): 200–16.

Wallace, R. J. (1996) *Responsibility and the Moral Sentiments* (Cambridge, Mass.: Harvard University Press).

Weale, A. (2005) *Democratic Citizenship and the European Union* (Manchester: Manchester University Press).

—— (2000a) 'Introduction', in A. Weale, G. Pridham, M. Cini, D. Konstadakopulos, M. Porter and B. Flynn, *Environmental Governance in Europe: An Ever Closer Ecological Union?* (Oxford: Oxford University Press).

—— (2000b) 'Government by Committee: Three Principles of Evaluation', in T. Christiansen and E. Kirchner (eds) *Committee Governance in the European Union* (Manchester: Manchester University Press).

Weale, A., and Lehning, P. (eds) (1997) *Citizenship, Democracy and Justice in the New Europe* (London: Routledge).

Weale, A., and Nentwich, M. (eds) (1998) *Political Theory and the European Union: Legitimacy, Constitutional Choice and Citizenship.* (London: Routledge).

Weber, M. [1919] (1978) 'Politics as a Vocation', in W. G. Runciman (ed.) *Weber: Selections in Translation* (Cambridge: Cambridge University Press).

Wessels, W. (1999) 'Comitology as a Research Subject: A New Legitimacy Mix?', in C. Joerges and E. Vos (eds) *EU Committees: Social Regulation, Law and Politics* (Oxford: Hart).

Westlake, M. (2006) 'The European Commission and the European Parliament', in E. Spence with G. Edwards (eds) *The European Commission* (London: John Harper).

Westlake, M., and Galloway, D. (2004) *The Council of the European Union*, 3rd edn (London: John Harper).

Wiener, A., and de la Sala, V. (1997) 'Constitution-Making and Citizenship Practice: Bridging the Democracy Gap in the EU', *Journal of Common Market Studies*, 35(4): 595–614.

Wincott, D. (1995) 'Institutional Interaction and European Integration: Towards an Everyday Critique of Liberal Intergovernmentalism', *Journal of Common Market Studies*, 33(4): 597–609.

Wind, M. (1997) 'Rediscovering Institutions: A Reflectivist Critique of Rational Institutionalism', in K. E. Joergensen (ed.) *Reflective Approaches to European Governance* (New York: St Martin's Press).

Index